Country Fresh Gifts

Recipes and Projects from Your Garden and Country Kitchen

From Storey's Country Wisdom Collection
The Editors of Storey Publishing

A Storey Publishing Book

STOREY

Storey Communications, Inc.
Schoolhouse Road
Pownal, Vermont 05261

Cover design by Wanda Harper
Cover illustrations by Alison Kolesar
Text design and production by Michelle Arabia
Edited by Cornelia M. Parkinson

Illustration Credits:
Introduction — Alison Kolesar and Mike Belanger
Chapter 1 — Mike Belanger and Nancy Anisfield
Chapter 2 — Mike Belanger and Nancy Anisfield
Chapter 3 — Sue Storey, Mike Belanger, James Blair, Brigita Fuhrmann and Charles Joslin
Chapter 4 — Nancy Anisfield and Mike Belanger
Chapter 5 — Nancy Anisfied and Mike Belanger
Chapter 6 — Mike Belanger
Chapter 7 — Mike Belanger
Chapter 8 — Alison Kolesar and Mike Belanger
Chapter 9 — Mike Belanger

Copyright © 1991 by Storey Communications, Inc.

First printing, June 1991

Printed in the United States by Courier

Library of Congress Cataloging-in-Publication Data

Country fresh gifts : recipes and projects from your garden and country kitchen : from
    Storey's country wisdom collection / the editors of Storey Publishing.
           p.   cm.
        "A Storey Publishing book."
        Includes index.
        ISBN 0-88266-660-6 (pb)
          1. Cookery.   2. Handicraft.   3. Gifts.   I. Storey Communications.
TX652.C77   1991
641.5—dc20   90-50606
                                          CIP

Table of Contents

Introduction

When we are deciding on gifts to give to friends and loved ones, there are usually several questions to be addressed. What can we give her/him/them? Will they *really* like it? Can we afford it? Could we — possibly — make it?

In *Country Fresh Gifts*, we present to you more than 200 ideas and recipes complete with instructions for making delightful, delectable, de-lovely foods, soaps, candles, potpourris, and flower arrangements, all from a country kitchen, all suitable for presentation as gifts.

You won't find any main menu recipes here, or picnic or potluck dishes. Recipes in this book are meant for joyous, casual gift-giving. This applies to your at-home family as well — wouldn't penuche or a batch of pretzels be nice for that tired man of the house, or the son or daughter who brings home a great report card? Maybe the teenagers will whip up a soft-scented jar of potpourri to soothe their working mother. We tell how to do it all.

Many ingredients can be homegrown. To get complete directions and tips for growing flowers and herbs, making cider, and all that, see our Country Wisdom bulletins. All recipes and instructions in this book, by the way, come from *Storey's Country Wisdom Collection.* See note at the end of each chapter for titles you'll want to own.

Gifts you make can be very personal, tailored to the recipient's tastes and preferences. Or you can introduce the new and unusual, like flavored vinegars or hazelnut liqueur. We've even included suggestions for packaging and materials. You'll think of dozens more.

What can you expect of *Country Fresh*

Gifts? We've made it easy for you, with an annotated table of contents and an index, with how-to illustrations, with topic headings in bold print, with recipe ingredients set off and in the order you'll need them, and clear directions for making those great breads and that remarkable wine. First, let us give you a preview.

Chapter 1, *Gifts from Garden and Orchard*, tells you how to make jams, jellies, conserves, marmalades, and butters. Unusual recipes are carrot jam, cinnamon basil jelly, and watermelon rind preserves. Your old favorites include apple butter, currant jelly, quince honey, and sun preserves (to be modern we say solar-cooked, but it's the same familiar sun).

Chapter 2, *Savories and Sauces*, includes pickles, relishes, salad dressings, and sauces. Try green tomato olives, or pickled peaches — they're a treat. Everything is there, from sweet gherkins to dills to pear chutney — even Oriental plum sauce. A troubleshooting column solves possible pickling problems.

Chapter 3, *Bottled Gifts,* tells you how to make wines, liqueurs, and flavored vinegars. How about some perry, or flower wine, or licorice liqueur or homemade Irish cream? You'll save some of those for yourselves! Vinegars include herb, fruit, and seven-pepper bases to perk up meats and salads.

Chapter 4 is *Gifts of Bread.* Featured (but not exclusive) are sourdough recipes and instructions for starting sourdough and keeping it alive. Among additional recipes are bagels, Englishstyle fruit scones, and lemon basil tea bread. For a snack, try sourdough sesame crackers.

Chapter 5 is *Just Desserts*, but it's not *merely* desserts. Everything is portable and delectable. Peach vinegar lends a subtle dimension to old-time vinegar pie. Our rhubarb-strawberry pie has both fruits. Squash pie, cherry cobbler, scented geranium cake — forget your diet. Like chocolate cake? Sourdough chocolate cake is more so. For a familiar treat, make gingerbread men.

Chapter 6, *Sweet Temptations*, is brimful of mouth-watering candies. Old friends — fudge, taffy, marzipan — are there. So are caraway comfits, truffles, and caramels. Make designer candies or hand-dipped chocolates, put liqueur in them or make specialties just for kids. The things you can *do* with buttercreams . . . .

Chapter 7, *Gifts of Light*, gets us into homemade soaps and candles. From our recipes you can make hard soap, kitchen soap, honey soap, and more. We tell how to make wicks, then explain how to mold, roll, or dip your candles for gifts or home use.

Chapter 8 is *Gifts of Flowers*. You'll learn more about arranging, drying, and preserving flowers than you ever dreamed of. Our tables name the flowers and plants to hang-dry, to dry in desiccant, to preserve in glycerine. Drawings show clearly how to arrange flowers formally. You'll find recipes and instructions for outstanding potpourris. Think about jasmine, Maine woods air, or spicy rose or bayberry potpourri for personal use or gift giving.

Wondering where to get some ingredient? See the list of suppliers, page 151.

Turn now to the first open page and start to browse. We know you'll enjoy *Country Fresh Gifts*, both in reading and making the recipes we've chosen for you, your family, and friends.

CHAPTER 1

Gifts from Garden and Orchard

"**D**ouble-spreading," our forefathers called it. Spread thick over butter on fresh homemade bread, jellies, jams, and preserves lift a meal out of the everyday into food for royalty. It makes the ideal gift.

Jelly is made from strained juices. It should be clear, colorful, firm enough to hold its shape, soft enough to spread easily.

To make jelly you'll need the following:

- A large enamel or stainless steel kettle
- Jars and lids
- Jelly bag or cheesecloth
- Potato or other masher
- Wooden stirring spoons
- Damp clean cloth
- Rack for cooling jars
- Measuring cups
- Candy thermometer
- Vegetable brush
- Paring knife
- Timer
- Slotted spoon

Steps in Jelly Making

1. Extract the juice. Slightly unripe fruit is best for jelly. Wash it. Pare only pineapple, core only quince. Cut up into kettle. Mash lower layer of berries. Add small amount of water only if fruit lacks enough juice to prevent scorching. Apples and plums require water. Start over low heat, gradually increasing heat as juice builds up. Cook until fruit is soft, about 3 minutes for berries, and 15 to 25 for harder fruit.

2. Strain juice. Put cooked fruit in damp jelly bag, and let juice drip into bowl.

Pressing or squeezing bag will cloud the jelly. Juice can be frozen or canned, and used later for making jelly.

A jelly bag can be made from four layers of cheesecloth which are tied at the four corners and suspended over a bowl, or place the layers of cheesecloth over a colander. In either case, dampen the cheesecloth before ladling the pulp into it.

3. Test for pectin. Put 1 tablespoon of juice in a glass. Add 1 tablespoon rubbing alcohol. Shake gently. *Don't taste*. Pectin should form a transparent glob, indicating high pectin content. Use equal amounts of juice and sugar in making jelly. If two or three globs form, pectin content is less, and you should use ⅔ to ¾ cup sugar to 1 cup juice. If smaller globs form, use ½

cup sugar to 1 cup juice. Pectin level can be raised by adding tart apple juice to juice prepared for making jelly.

Some juices such as apple and crab apple, cranberry, quince, gooseberry, and red currant, are high in the pectin so essential for jellies to jell. Low-pectin fruits include raspberries, blueberries, strawberries, blackberries, apricots, peaches, pears, cherries, and grapes. High-pectin fruits, particularly underripe apples, are often combined with low-pectin fruits to make jellies.

Other recipes call for the addition of commercial pectin. Liquid pectin is added after the sugar has been added to the juice and the combination has been brought to a boil. Powdered pectin is added to the unheated, unsweetened juice. Use the type pectin called for in the recipe; for example, don't use powdered pectin if liquid pectin is called for. Recipes calling for added pectin require more sugar; those without added pectin have to be cooked longer to reach the jelly stage.

4. Cook to jelly stage. Measure juice into kettle. Simmer 5 minutes in open kettle. Skim off froth. Add sugar. Boil rapidly.

5. Test for jelly stage. Jelling point (use candy thermometer) is 220° F. (or 8 degrees above boiling temperature for water where you live). Or let jelly drip off spoon. Jelly point is reached when jelly comes off spoon in a sheet. Begin testing 10 minutes after boiling starts. When ready, remove from heat, skim off foam with slotted spoon.

Pitfalls

CLOUDY JELLY
Juice not properly strained
Jelly bag was squeezed
Too much unripe fruit
Delayed pouring into jars
Overcooking

STIFF JELLY
Too much pectin
Overcooking

WEAK JELLY
Insufficient pectin
Too much water
Not enough acid
Cooked in too large amounts

Note: Additional cooking or more pectin sometimes will remedy this.

SPOILED JELLY
Too little sugar
Improper sealing

BUBBLES
Improper pouring
Improper sealing

FLOATING FRUIT (JAMS AND PRESERVES)
Too much unripe fruit
Insufficient cooking

CRYSTAL FORMATION
Improper cooking; too long, too short, too slowly
Too much sugar

6. Seal the jelly. Ladle or pour the hot jelly into hot, sterilized containers.

Leave ¼ inch headroom. Wipe rim with a clean damp cloth to remove any jelly that could spoil seal. Take self-sealing lids from hot water and place on jar. Screw the band on tightly.

If jelly can't be stored in 50° F. temperature or less, we recommend using canning jars and giving them the boiling-water treatment. Place closed jar in rack in simmering water. Add water to bring it 2 inches above the tops of the jars. Put on cover, bring water to a full rolling boil, and time for just 5 minutes. Remove jars immediately, and place on rack to cool.

7. And finally . . . let cool, label, and store in a cold, dry place (32° to 50° F.) is ideal.

Berry Jelly

(Blackberry, black raspberry, dewberry, elderberry, loganberry, red raspberry, strawberry, youngberry)

3 quarts berries
7½ cups sugar
1 bottle liquid pectin

Wash and crush berries. Extract juice by using a jelly bag. Measure 4 cups juice into kettle. Add sugar. Bring to full boil, stirring constantly. Reduce heat and add pectin. Reheat to full boil and stir for one minute. Remove from heat, skim, and ladle into hot glasses and seal.

Note: ¼ cup lemon juice may be added to blackberry, elderberry, and black raspberry mixtures.

Makes eight 8-ounce glasses.

Apple or Crab Apple Jelly

(Without Pectin)

4 pounds apples
4 cups water
3 cups sugar

Use hard, tart fruit. Wash apples, discard stems and blossom ends. Cut apples into small chunks. Place in kettle. Add 1 cup water per pound of apples. Bring to a boil and simmer 25 minutes. Place fruit and juice in suspended cheesecloth jelly bag. Allow juice to drip overnight. In the morning, measure 4 cups of juice into kettle, add sugar, heat, and stir until sugar dissolves. Bring to a boil and cook rapidly until jelly test is met. Skim off foam. Pour into hot, sterilized glasses. Adjust lids and process.

Makes four to five 8-ounce glasses.

Sour Cherry Jelly

3 pounds red sour cherries
½ cup water
7 cups sugar
1 bottle liquid pectin

Wash, stem, and crush fruit. Add water and bring to a boil. Reduce heat and simmer 10 to 12 minutes. Extract juice with a jelly bag. Combine 3 cups juice and sugar. Heat until sugar is dissolved. Bring to a boil and remove from heat. Add pectin. Stir and remove scum. Pour into hot, sterilized glasses. Adjust lids and process.

Makes about seven 8-ounce glasses.

Currant Jelly and Bar-Le-Duc (Jam)

3 quarts currants
2 cups water
3 cups sugar

Wash and stem currants (stemming unnecessary if making only jelly). Add water and heat to boiling. Reduce heat and simmer 10 minutes. Extract juice by means of jelly bag. Allow juice to drip overnight. Reserve pulp for jam-making.

Measure 4 cups juice and stir in 3 cups sugar. Heat to boiling. Continue cooking and stirring for 5 minutes until mixture meets the jelly test. (Currants are high in natural pectin.) Skim and pour into glasses and seal. Process 5 minutes in a boiling-water bath.

Makes four 8-ounce glasses.

Bar-Le-Duc (currant jam) may be made from the reserved pulp and any excess juice. For every cup of pulp add ¾ cup sugar and cook (syrup is thick) until desired consistency is reached.

Makes 2 half-pints.

Cinnamon Basil Jelly

1½ cups cinnamon basil leaves
2¼ cups cold water
3 tablespoons lemon juice
3½ cups sugar
One 3-ounce pouch liquid pectin

    Finely chop the basil and place in a saucepan with 2¼ cups cold water. Bring to a full boil, cover, remove from the heat, and allow the mixture to steep for 15 minutes. Pour the mixture into a jelly bag or a fine strainer and let it drip. There should be about 1¾ cups of basil "tea."

    Put the basil "tea" into a large saucepan along with the lemon juice and sugar. Cook the mixture over high heat, stirring constantly until the mixture comes to a full rolling boil (a boil that can't be stirred down). Boil for 1 minute, then remove from the heat. Stir in the pectin and ladle the liquid jelly into sterilized half-pint jars. Wipe the rims of the jars clean and seal with proper lids. Turn the jars upside down for 30 minutes to seal the lids, then turn them right side up and allow the jelly to set and cool.

Makes 4 half-pints.

Adapted from *Growing & Using Basil.*

Cranberry Jelly

(Without Pectin)

2½ pints berries
1½ cups water
2½ cups sugar

    Cover berries with water and cook uncovered until berries soften. Put mixture through food mill. Add sugar and cook until mixture meets jelly test (about 3 minutes).

    Since cranberry jelly has a tendency to "weep," it is frequently poured into molds and not unmolded until it is served.

    Note: Add 1 teaspoon ground cinnamon, ½ teaspoon ground cloves and allspice if spiced jelly is desired.

Makes about three 8-ounce glasses.

Herb Jellies

Herb jellies may be made of one or a combination of herbs, or in combination with apple jelly. Try both ways. We prefer fresh herbs, but dried ones may be used. Use half as much dried herbs as the fresh herb recipe specifies. Try any of these herbs: basil, lemon verbena, marjoram, mint, parsley, rosemary, sage, tarragon, or thyme.

1 cup fresh herbs (leaves and stems)
2½ cups boiling water
4½ cups sugar
¼ cup lemon juice or vinegar
½ bottle liquid pectin

Make an infusion by steeping herbs in boiling water for 20 minutes. Add sugar and lemon juice. Heat until sugar dissolves. Bring mixture to a boil and add pectin. Boil for 1 minute, stirring constantly. Remove from heat and skim. Place a few fresh herb leaves in each jelly glass. Pour and seal. Process 5 minutes in a boiling-water bath.

Makes four 8-ounce glasses.

Green Pepper Jelly

6 green peppers
1½ cups cider vinegar
6 cups sugar
½ teaspoon salt
1 teaspoon crushed red pepper
1 bottle pectin

Remove seeds and stems, and cut peppers into small pieces. Mix with vinegar, then liquefy in blender (it will take two batches in blender). Pour into pan and add sugar, salt, and red pepper. Bring to a boil. Add pectin. Boil until it passes test for jelling. Pour into sterilized, hot jars and seal. Process 5 minutes in a boiling-water bath.

Makes four 8-ounce glasses.
Excellent with meats and fish.

Herb-Apple Jelly

2 cups apple juice
½ cup herb leaves
¾ cup sugar

Combine ingredients. Heat until sugar dissolves and mixture meets jelly test. Pour into hot glasses and seal. Process 5 minutes in a boiling-water bath.

Makes two 8-ounce glasses.

Jams

Jams are made from crushed fruit with or without added pectin. This is one of the most economical fruit concoctions to make, since it calls for but one cooking, and even the pulp of the fruit is used.

Making it is simple. Wash the fruit. Prepare it by cutting hard fruits into small pieces, and crushing soft fruits. Measure the amount. Put it into the kettle. Add the sugar or honey. Bring it to a boil, stirring frequently so it doesn't scorch. When it reaches 221° F. (or 9 degrees above the boiling point of water in your area) it's cooked. This may take as much as a half-hour. Remove it from the heat, skim off the foam, and stir jam for about five minutes, letting the jam cool. This prevents fruit from floating to the top of the jam.

Process them for 5 minutes in a boiling-water bath.

Solar-Cooked Jams

Cherry, strawberry, and raspberry jams may be sun-cooked. This process requires full sun and some patience since the preserves should be made in small batches.

3 pounds prepared fruit
3 pounds sugar
¾ cup water

Wash and hull berries; pit cherries. Layer fruit and sugar and let sit for 20 to 30 minutes; add water. Heat and stir until sugar is dissolved.

Pour mixture in batches into shallow baking dishes or platters. Cover with glass, plastic wrap, or cheesecloth to deter curious and voracious insects. Jelling depends upon the weather. The entire process may take several days. The platters should be brought inside when late-afternoon sun loses its potency. If you weary of this adventure, finish cooking on the stove.

Rosy Rhubarb and Pineapple Jam

2 cups rhubarb
One 20-ounce can crushed pineapple
1 teaspoon orange peel, grated
½ teaspoon lemon peel, grated
2 tablespoons lemon juice
6 cups sugar
½ bottle liquid pectin
Red food coloring

Combine first five ingredients in an enamelware saucepan. Add sugar and mix well. Stirring constantly, bring mixture to a rolling boil; continue stirring and cooking for 1 minute.

Remove from heat and stir in pectin and drops of food coloring, if desired. Skim off foam and stir jam, allowing it to cool for 10 minutes.

Ladle mixture into sterilized jars and seal. Process 5 minutes in a boiling-water bath.

Makes 3 pints.
Adapted from *Great Rhubarb Recipes*.

Carrot Jam

3 cups carrots, chopped
2½ cups sugar
Juice of 2 lemons
Rind of 2 lemons, grated
1 teaspoon cinnamon
½ teaspoon cloves

Combine ingredients. Mix well. Heat slowly, stirring frequently, and simmer until mixture thickens.

Pour into hot, sterilized jars and seal. Process 5 minutes in a boiling-water bath.

Makes five 8-ounce jars.

Mulberry Jam

4 pounds berries, stemmed
½ cup salt dissolved in 2 quarts water
6 cups sugar
Juice of one lemon
1 teaspoon ground cinnamon

Cover berries with salt water and let stand 8 minutes. Drain berries and rinse three times. Place in saucepan. Crush berries and simmer gently, stirring frequently, until soft. Add sugar, lemon juice, and cinnamon. Cook for 20 minutes or until desired consistency is reached.

Ladle into hot, sterilized jars and seal. Process 5 minutes in a boiling-water bath.

Makes 3 to 4 pints.

Peach Melba Jam

4 cups prepared peaches
2 cups ripe red raspberries
Juice of one lemon
6 cups sugar
½ bottle liquid pectin

Peel and pit peaches. Chop and crush. Blend with raspberries. Crush mixture. Add lemon juice and sugar. Bring mixture to boil and stir until heated through, about 1 minute. Remove from heat. Add pectin. Mix thoroughly. Stir and skim for several minutes.

Ladle into hot, sterilized jars and seal. Process 5 minutes in a boiling-water bath.

Makes ten 8-ounce jars.

Rose Hip Jam

4 cups rose hip puree
5 cups sugar
1 tablespoon lemon juice

Collect hips after the first frost. Prepare puree by covering hips with water and simmering until they are soft. Put pulp through food mill. Combine pulp, sugar, and lemon juice. Bring to a boil; reduce heat. Simmer until desired consistency is reached. Ladle into hot, sterilized jars and seal. Process 5 minutes in a boiling-water bath.

Makes 2 to 3 pints.

Scuppernong Jam

5 pounds grapes
Water
6 pounds sugar

Wash and stem grapes. Slip skins from pulp. Simmer skins for 15 minutes in small amount of water to prevent sticking. Simmer pulp until it softens and put it through a food mill to remove seeds. Combine skin and pulp with sugar. Cook over low heat, stirring frequently until sugar dissolves. Note: One tablespoon each of ground cloves and cinnamon may be added if spiced jam is preferred. Bring to a full boil, reduce heat, let simmer and stir until mixture reaches desired consistency.

Ladle into hot, sterilized jars and seal. Process 5 minutes in a boiling-water bath.

Makes 6 pints.

Butters

Butters are much like jams. They should be thick, but easily spreadable. During cooking, keep heat low and stir frequently to avoid burning.

Butters should be kept in canning jars, to insure a good seal and a long storage life. Ladle butter into sterilized jar, leaving ¼ inch headroom, quickly take lids from hot water and place on jar, then screw band on tightly. Process in boiling-water bath by putting jars in kettle of simmering water, adding enough water to bring level 2 inches over tops of the jars, putting on cover, bringing water to a full rolling boil, and timing for just 5 minutes. Remove jars immediately and place on rack to cool.

Baked Apple Butter

5 pounds apples
2 cups apple cider
5 cups sugar
1 teaspoon nutmeg
1 teaspoon ground cloves
½ teaspoon allspice
1 teaspoon ground cinnamon

Place unpeeled, quartered apples in kettle and add cider. Cook 20 minutes or until soft. Put pulp through food mill. Add seasonings and mix well. Pour mixture into casserole or other container suitable for baking. Bake at 300° F. until desired consistency is reached. This may take several hours. Stir occasionally. Overcooking will result in stiff butter. Butter should be thick but moist. Ladle into hot, sterilized jars, leaving ¼ inch headroom, seal, and process in boiling-water bath for 5 minutes.

Blueberry Conserve

1 cup water
8 cups blueberries, washed
8 cups sugar
1 lemon, ground, plus juice
1 orange, ground, plus juice
1 cup seedless raisins
¼ teaspoon ground allspice
¼ teaspoon ground cinnamon
⅛ teaspoon ground cloves

Combine all ingredients and cook gently until berry skins are tender and mixture has reached desired consistency.

Ladle into sterilized jars, seal, and process in boiling-water bath for 5 minutes.

Makes five 8-ounce jars.

Conserves

These delightful combinations of two or more fruits, and sometimes nuts and raisins, are a delicious addition to any meal. They should be ladled into hot, sterilized canning jars, sealed, and processed in a boiling-water bath for 5 minutes. (See Butters.)

Fruit Razzle Dazzle

8 cups sugar

1 cup water

Any 4 of the following:

1 pint cherries

1 pint strawberries

1 pint rhubarb

1 pint currants

1 pint gooseberries

1 pint raspberries

Combine sugar and water. Cook until sugar thoroughly dissolves. Add fruit and simmer mixture 20 minutes.

Ladle into hot, sterilized canning jars, seal, and process in a boiling-water bath for 5 minutes.

Makes about 4 pints.

Plum Conserve

Add 1 seeded chopped orange and lemon (peel and all), 1 cup seedless raisins and 1 cup chopped nuts to the Plum Preserves recipe (page 15), adding nuts just before conserve reaches desired consistency.

Makes 7 to 8 pints.

Grape Conserve

4 pounds Concord grapes

4 cups sugar

⅓ teaspoon salt

1 orange

1 cup nuts, chopped

Slip skins from grapes and set aside. Simmer grape pulp for 15 minutes to loosen seeds. Remove seeds by forcing pulp through sieve or food mill. Remove seeds from orange and chop, unpeeled. Combine grape pulp, seasonings, and orange. Stirring frequently, heat mixture until it begins to thicken. Add grape skins and cook 10 to 15 minutes longer until desired consistency is reached. Add nuts.

Pour conserve into sterilized jars, seal, and process in boiling-water bath for 5 minutes.

Makes about eight 8-ounce jars.

Marmalades

These are jellies with small pieces of fruit held in jellied suspension. When cooked, they are brought almost to the point of jellying. They should be ladled into hot, sterilized jars, sealed, and processed in a boiling-water bath for 5 minutes. (See Step 6, page 4.)

Pinchberry (Wild Cherry) Marmalade

2 oranges

1½ quarts wild cherries

3 cups sugar

3 tablespoons lemon juice

Remove the orange outer peeling with a potato peeler. Set aside. Remove and discard white membrane from orange. Chop orange pulp, combine with rind strips, cover with water, and simmer until rind is soft. Add pitted cherries, sugar, and lemon juice. Cook until mixture meets jelly test. Pour into hot sterilized jars, seal, and process in boiling-water bath for 5 minutes.

Makes about six 8-ounce jars.

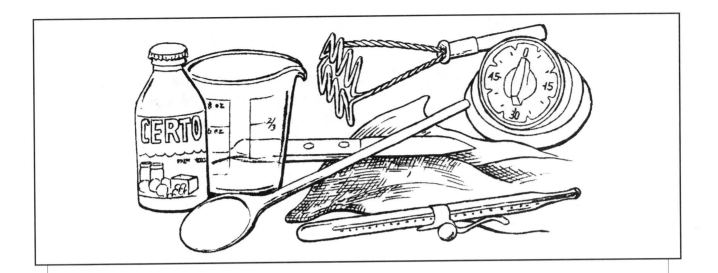

Green Tomato Marmalade

24 medium green tomatoes
4 oranges
3½ pounds granulated sugar

Core and peel green tomatoes and cut in thin slices. Wash and peel oranges and cut peeling into thin strips. Cut oranges into thin slices. Combine tomato slices, peeling and orange slices with sugar in a kettle and let stand overnight. In the morning, place kettle over low heat and gradually bring mixture to a boil, stirring occasionally. Simmer gently about two hours, until thick. Pour immediately into hot, sterilized jelly jars and seal. Process 5 minutes in a boiling-water bath.

Makes 6 pints.

Adapted from *52 Great Green Tomato Recipes*.

Quince Honey

2 cups sugar
⅔ cup water
2 cups quince, grated

Dissolve sugar in water over low heat. Peel and grate quince. Add to sugar mixture and cook until thickened. Pour into hot, sterilized jars, seal, and process in boiling-water bath for 5 minutes.

Makes two to three 8-ounce jars.

Red Raspberry Marmalade

2 oranges
2 lemons
½ cup water
⅛ teaspoon baking soda
4 cups raspberries
7 cups sugar
1 bottle liquid pectin

Grate the orange and lemon rinds; reserve. Juice the citrus fruit, chop pulp. Combine rind, water, and soda. Simmer 12 to 15 minutes. Add chopped citrus pulp and juice. Continue cooking 15 more minutes. Crush berries and add to mixture. Heat and mix thoroughly. Add sugar and continue cooking gently until sugar is dissolved. Remove from heat. Add pectin, stir and skim for one minute.

Ladle into sterilized jars, seal, and process in boiling-water bath for 5 minutes.

Makes about five 8-ounce jars.

Preserves

Fruit retains its shape in preserves, and is clear and shiny. The aim is to have clear syrup, as thick as honey, or thicker — almost to the point of jelling. Syrup may not reach — or may pass — that stage. If syrup is too watery when fruit has reached the clear, shiny stage, remove the fruit with a slotted spoon, place it in hot, sterilized jars, then continue to cook syrup until it reaches the desired consistency. If it is too thick, add small amounts (¼ cup at a time) of boiling water to delay the syrup reaching the jelling point before the fruit is clear.

All preserves should be processed in boiling-water bath for 5 minutes. (See Step 6, page 4.)

Cherry Preserves

5 pounds cherries
4 pounds sugar

Wash, stem, and pit cherries. Layer fruit in kettle with sugar, ending with a layer of sugar on top. Allow mixture to stand overnight. In the morning, bring to a boil, stirring frequently. Allow mixture to simmer for 30 minutes until fruit is tender and sugar is dissolved. If a thicker consistency is desired, strain off juice, reheat it, and cook until it thickens, or add ½ bottle pectin. Ladle into hot sterilized jars, seal, and process in boiling-water bath for 5 minutes.

Makes 4 pints.

Note: For spiced preserves add ½ teaspoon each of ground cinnamon and cloves before boiling.

Cranberry Preserves

2 quarts cranberries
3 cups water
2⅔ cups sugar

Combine berries and water. Cook until skins burst. Add sugar, heating and stirring until sugar is dissolved. With slotted spoon, ladle berries into hot, sterilized jars. Continue cooking syrup until it thickens. Pour over berries, seal jars, and process in boiling-water bath for 5 minutes.

Conserve can be made by adding 1 cup seeded raisins, 1 teaspoon each of ground cloves, cinnamon, and allspice.

Makes 4 half-pints.

Plum Preserves (Blue Damson)

12 cups prepared plums
¾ cup water
8 cups sugar

Wash fruit. Cut in half and discard pits. Combine plums with water and sugar. Simmer, stirring frequently, until sugar is dissolved. Bring mixture to a boil, stirring constantly; continue cooking until mixture reaches desired consistency.

Ladle into sterilized jars, seal, and process in boiling-water bath for 5 minutes.

Makes twelve 8-ounce jars.

Tomato-Pear Preserves

1 orange
2 lemons
3 pounds tomatoes (small and firm)
2 pounds pears
5 cups sugar
2 tablespoons crystallized ginger

Squeeze orange and lemons; reserve juice. Cut citrus peel into narrow strips. Cover with water, bring to a boil, reduce heat, and simmer 15 minutes. Drain. Scald tomatoes and remove skins. Peel and core pears and slice. Combine lemon juice, peels, tomatoes, pears, and remaining ingredients. Heat to boiling. Reduce heat and simmer until desired consistency is reached, about 2 hours.

Ladle into hot, sterilized jars, seal, and process 5 minutes in boiling-water bath.

Makes 4 pints.

Watermelon Rind Preserves

3 pints watermelon rind, prepared
2 quarts of water in which are dissolved 4 tablespoons salt
2 cups ice water
1 tablespoon ground ginger
4 cups sugar
¼ cup lemon juice
7 cups water
1 lemon, sliced

Remove fruit and green from rind. Cut rind into 1-inch cubes and soak overnight in salt water. Drain and soak again in ice water for 2 hours. Drain. Spread ginger over rind, cover with water and cook until tender.

Combine sugar, lemon juice, and 7 cups water. Boil until sugar is dissolved, add drained rind and boil for a half-hour, then add sliced lemon and cook until melon rind is clear. Ladle into hot, sterilized jars, seal, and process in boiling-water bath for 5 minutes.

Makes 3 pints.

Strawberry Preserves

3 pints strawberries
5 cups sugar
1½ cups lemon juice

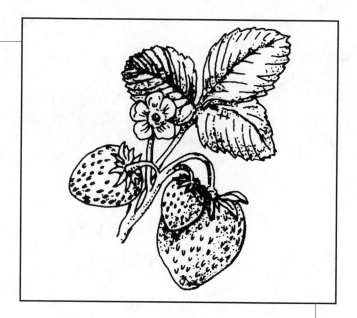

Wash and stem berries. Add sugar and let strawberries combine with it for 4 hours. Bring to boiling, stirring, and add lemon juice. Cook until berries are clear and syrup reaches desired consistency. Pour into a shallow pan and let cool overnight. Ladle into hot, sterilized jars, seal, and process in boiling-water bath for 5 minutes.

Makes about 4 half-pint jars.

Except as noted, material in this chapter has been excerpted and adapted from Jams, Jellies & Preserves, *Storey/Garden Way Publishing Country Wisdom Bulletin #A-32.*

CHAPTER 2

Savories and Sauces

Pickles, Relishes, Dressings

Whether sweetly piquant, mouth-puckeringly sour, or flaming hot and pungent, pickles and relishes bring zest to the table. They enliven mundane meals, brighten salads, add panache to picnics and potlucks, and provide very special gifts. And with modern methods, it takes just a few kitchen hours to transform the seasonal bounty of your garden into a year-round source of pickled delicacies.

Most of the recipes here are for fresh-pack pickles: produce prepared and packed raw into jars. Often vegetables are short-brined — salted and allowed to stand for a few hours — before packing. This makes them crisp. Then a boiling syrup or brine is poured over them. The jars are sealed and processed in a canner, unless they are to be refrigerated or frozen.

Also included are recipes for traditional brined pickles, the ones you used to find in big crocks at the general store. In this method the vegetables are cured

several weeks in brine before being packed into jars and processed or refrigerated. Brining, a fermentation process, works best at 70° to 80° F. Bacteria generate lactic acid from sugars in the vegetables, giving the cured pickles a distinct, sharp flavor.

Ingredients

The difference between a good pickle and a great one is usually the freshness of the ingredients. Select young or even slightly immature, unbruised fruits and vegetables. Ideally, harvest early in the day, before the sun wilts them, and process immediately. Since this isn't always possible, chill your produce quickly and thoroughly to ensure a crisp pickle. This is particularly important with cucumbers. If you don't have a garden, buy from local farmers, roadside stands, or farmers' markets. If you must buy from the supermarket, avoid fruits and vegetables that have been waxed. No matter where it comes from, always wash and drain produce thoroughly before use.

Cucumbers come in two types, pickling and slicing. A good pickling cucumber is thin-skinned and small. It may be warty. Slicing cucumbers, when still small, are acceptable for sliced pickles such as bread and butters, and they are fine in relishes, but they rarely make good dills. For the inevitable overgrown cucumbers hiding in the garden, try the recipe for honey spears on page 22. Relishes are also a "forgiving pickle." You can frequently use slightly overgrown or undermature produce with good results.

Most pickle recipes call for vinegar, salt, herbs and spices, water, and a sweetener. It is best to use commercially made vinegars. To safely preserve pickles, the vinegar must have 4 to 6 percent acetic acid, and homemade vinegar may not be strong enough. For the same reason, never reduce the amount of vinegar in a recipe. White vinegar is most commonly used because it does not color the pickle. Cider vinegar has a rich, somewhat mellow flavor and less bite. It is preferred for many sweet pickle and chutney recipes. Malt vinegar, with a delicate, almost sweet flavor, is used in a few recipes. While you may substitute one vinegar for another, keep in mind that it will change the flavor. Salt both flavors and preserves. It preserves first by drawing water from the food to make it crisper, and second, by creating a hostile environment for microorganisms. Always use pure pickling salt or dairy salt, and do measure exactly.

The traditional pickling herbs and spices are dill, mustard seeds, celery seeds, garlic, pepper, cloves, and prepackaged mixed pickling slices. But the seasoning possibilities are endless, and recipes here include summer savory, basil, fennel, coriander, tarragon, hot pepper, and nutmeg, to name just a few. Herbs and spices must be fresh, and they should be whole rather than ground, if you want a clear brine. Many recipes call for tying them into a cloth bag for easy removal. Cheesecloth, muslin, and stainless steel teaballs work well, too.

Equipment

Always use stainless steel, glass, or ceramic pans, bowls, and utensils. The salts and acids in pickles react with metals to produce an off-flavor. A food processor is a great timesaver and gives uniform results, thus improving the texture of the pickle.

Mason jars with two-piece lids are the most readily available canning jars. The dome lids cannot be reused, but the screwbands can. It is a good idea to remove them once the jar is sealed. Bail-wire jars are no longer recommended. (Whichever you use, always follow manufacturer's directions in preparing for canning.) For slow-brined pickles, glass, plastic, or ceramic crocks are useful. To prepare, wash well in soapy water, rinse, then scald with boiling water.

Canners

The United States Department of Agriculture recommends processing pickles in a boiling-water bath canner. They have tested the method and found it safe for high-acid foods. The USDA does not recommend use of a steam canner.

Pickling Tips

When packing jars, a widemouth funnel and wooden spoon pack vegetables neatly and firmly. Run a chopstick or spatula between food and side of jar to remove trapped bubbles. Add more brine if necessary to correct head space. Yields are approximate: have an extra jar or two ready.

After processing, place jars on a towel or wooden rack in a draft-free place. Cool undisturbed for 24 hours, then test seals. On screw-band jars, the lid center should be depressed and not pop back. Refrigerate unsealed jars and use within two weeks.

To store, wash, label, and date jars. Keep in a dark, dry cupboard between 32° and 50° F. to avoid vitamin loss and fading. Most pickles should be stored at least 6 weeks to develop flavor.

For slow-brined pickles: Hold cucumbers under brine with a weighted plate. Fermentation should begin within 2 days. Taste occasionally to see if pickles are sour enough for you. Refrigeration halts curing. Fermentation is complete when gas bubbles stop rising to top of crock, between second and fourth week. Tap crock side when checking for bubbles.

Where a recipe does not require processing in a canner, then the pickles are refrigerated or frozen instead. Most of these can be found under the heading "Refrigerator and Freezer Pickles"; those appearing elsewhere are marked with an asterisk (*).

What Went Wrong?

PROBLEM	CAUSE
• Soft or Slippery Pickles	Scum not skimmed from surface daily (slow brining)
	• Pickles not well covered by brine
	• Jars stored in a warm place
	• Water too hard
	• Blossom end not sliced
	• Jars did not seal properly
	Brine too strong
• Shriveled Pickles	• Syrup too sweet
	• Vinegar too strong
	• Cucumbers not fresh
	Water too hard
• Dark Pickles	• Used copper, brass, galvanized metal, or iron equipment
	• Canning lids corroded
	• Cucumbers lacking in nitrogen
	Cucumbers over-mature or sunburned
• Hollow Pickles	
	Proper head space not maintained
• Lids Didn't Seal	• Nonstandard jars or lids used
	• Jars not sufficiently processed
	• Jar rim not wiped well

Sweet Gherkins

5 quarts cucumbers, 1½ to 3 inches in
  length (about 7 pounds)
½ cup pickling salt
8 cups sugar
6 cups white vinegar
¾ teaspoon turmeric
2 teaspoons celery seeds
2 teaspoons mixed pickling spices
Eight 1-inch cinnamon sticks
½ teaspoon fennel (optional)

First day. Morning: Wash cucumbers thoroughly; scrub with vegetable brush; stem ends may be left on. Drain; place in large container and cover with boiling water. Afternoon (6 to 8 hours later): Drain; cover with fresh, boiling water.

Second day. Morning: Drain; cover with fresh, boiling water. Afternoon: Drain; add salt; cover with fresh, boiling water.

Third day. Morning: Drain; prick cucumbers in several places with a table fork. Make a syrup of 3 cups sugar and 3 cups vinegar; add turmeric and spices. Heat to boiling and pour over cucumbers. (The cucumbers will be partially covered at this point.) Afternoon: Drain syrup into pan; add 2 cups sugar and 2 cups vinegar. Heat to boiling and pour over pickles.

Fourth day. Morning: Drain syrup into pan; add 2 cups sugar and 1 cup vinegar. Heat to boiling and pour over pickles. Afternoon: Drain syrup into pan; add remaining 1 cup sugar; heat to boiling. Pack pickles into clean, hot pint jars and cover with boiling syrup, leaving ½ inch headspace. Seal. Process for 5 minutes in a boiling-water bath canner.

Yield: 7 to 8 pints.

Quick Mustard Pickles

1½ cups white vinegar
1 cup water
1 cup sugar
½ cup prepared mustard
2 teaspoons pickling salt
1 teaspoon prepared horseradish
8 cups cucumbers, sliced or cut in ½-inch
  chunks

In a large saucepan, combine all but cucumbers and bring to a boil. Pack cucumbers into hot, sterilized pint jars. Add boiling liquid, leaving ½ inch headspace. Seal. Process in a boiling-water bath canner for 5 minutes.

Yield: 4 pints.

Bread and Butter Pickles

25 cucumbers, sliced medium thick (about
 10 pounds)
1⅓ cups pickling salt
5 cups white vinegar
5 cups sugar
2 teaspoons mustard seeds
1 teaspoon powdered cloves

In a large glass, ceramic, or stainless steel bowl combine cucumbers and salt and let stand for 3 hours. Then drain.

In a medium-size saucepan, combine remaining ingredients and bring to a boil. Add cucumbers, but do not reboil.

Pack cucumbers and syrup into hot, sterilized pint jars, leaving ½ inch headspace. Seal. Process in a boiling-water bath canner for 5 minutes.

Yield: 7 to 8 pints.

Indian Pickles

8 medium green tomatoes, cored
8 medium ripe tomatoes, cored and
 peeled
3 medium onions, peeled
3 sweet red peppers, cored and seeded
1 large cucumber
7 cups celery, chopped
⅔ cup flaked pickling salt
6 cups vinegar
6 cups brown sugar
1 teaspoon dry mustard
1 teaspoon white pepper

Coarsely chop all vegetables. Sprinkle with salt and let stand overnight. In the morning, drain, discarding liquid. Combine with remaining ingredients in an open kettle. Place over low heat and bring to the simmering point slowly. Cook 30 minutes, stirring occasionally. Pack into hot, sterilized jars, leaving ½ inch headspace, and seal at once. Process 10 minutes in boiling-water bath.

Makes 5 to 6 pints.

Adapted from *52 Great Green Tomato Recipes*.

Honey Spears

12 large ripe cucumbers, peeled and seeded
6 large onions, sliced
½ cup pickling salt
1 gallon water
3 cups cider vinegar
1 cup water
2 cups honey or maple syrup
2 tablespoons mustard seeds
2 teaspoons celery seeds
2 teaspoons turmeric

Slice cucumbers into spears. Combine salt and water in a large glass, ceramic, or stainless steel bowl. Add cucumbers and onions and soak overnight.

The next morning, combine remaining ingredients in a large kettle and cook for 5 minutes. Add drained cucumbers and onions. Heat to boiling. Ladle mixture into clean, hot pint jars, leaving ½ inch headspace. Seal. Process in a boiling-water bath canner for 10 minutes.

Yield: 5 to 6 pints.

Sour Pickles

2 quarts cider vinegar
½ cup dry mustard
5 cups sugar
1 cup pickling salt
60 to 80 scrubbed tiny cucumbers (1½ to 2½ inches long) or larger ones cut into chunks or spears

Combine vinegar, mustard, sugar, and salt. Pour into a clean gallon jar or container. Add cucumbers. Let stand for 7 days in a cool place.

Drain and save brine. Pack pickles in clean, hot pint jars. Fill with saved brine to cover. Leave ½ inch headspace. Seal. Process for 15 minutes in a preheated boiling-water bath canner.

Yield: 7 to 8 pints.

Dill Pickles

*Andrea's 3-Day Deli Dills

This is a recipe for half-sour dills. Very delicious.

1 gallon small pickling cucumbers
8 cups water
¼ cup pickling salt
4 cloves garlic
4 bay leaves
6 dill heads
2 tablespoons dill seeds
8 grape leaves

Wash cucumbers. Remove blossom ends. Pack in a gallon jar. Combine the water and salt. Stir to dissolve. Add the garlic cloves, bay leaves, dill heads and seeds, and grape leaves to the jar. Pour brine over cucumbers. Cover with a weight to keep cucumbers below brine. Store at room temperature. If a scum forms, remove it daily. Pickles are done in about 3 days.

Pour off brine. Bring it to a boil. Cool. Pack pickles in clean quart jars. Pour brine over pickles. Store in refrigerator.

Yield: 4 quarts.

*Cured Dill Pickles

Here's a traditional recipe for brined dill pickles.

15 to 20 grape leaves
10 to 12 dill heads
1 ounce mixed pickling spices (4 scant
    tablespoons)
3½ gallons cucumbers (about 20 pounds)
1 pound pickling salt
2 cups white vinegar
2 gallons water

Scald and cool a 4-gallon stone jar or crock. Line the bottom with half the grape leaves, then add a layer of half the dill and ½ ounce of mixed pickling spices. Fill to within 2 or 3 inches of the top with washed cucumbers of as nearly the same size as possible. Add another ½ ounce mixed pickling spices and another layer of dill. Then cover with the rest of the grape leaves.

Make a brine of the salt, vinegar, and water. Bring to a boil. Cool. Pour over the cucumbers. Cover with a board or plate and put a weight on it to hold cucumbers (and grape leaves) well below brine.

If the temperature is maintained at around 86° F., active fermentation will begin at once and will be completed in 10 to 14 days. Fermentation will take longer at lower temperatures. Remove scum from surface daily.

As soon as the cucumbers are sufficiently cured, which may be determined by their agreeable flavor and dark green color, and after active fermentation has stopped, protect pickles against spoilage by making a fresh brine. Bring it to a boil and cool. Then pack pickles into sterilized jars, add a few fresh dill heads, and pour in brine.

Store in refrigerator.

Yield: 3½ gallons.

Easy Green Tomato Dills

Wash small green cherry tomatoes but do not peel or core. Pack loosely in quart canning jars. To each jar add:

1 peeled garlic clove
½ teaspoon mixed pickling spices
1 sprig fresh dill
1 small piece hot red pepper (optional)

In a saucepan, combine:
2 quarts water
2 cups vinegar
1 cup flaked pickling salt

Bring to a boil and stir to dissolve salt. Pour over tomatoes in jars to within ½ inch of tops. Seal jars at once. Let set 6 weeks to cure before eating.
Keep refrigerated after opening.

Adapted from 52 Great Green Tomato Recipes.

*Freezer Tarragon Pickles

8 cups sliced cucumbers
2 medium-size onions, sliced
2 tablespoons pickling salt
1 cup white sugar
½ cup wine vinegar
½ cup white vinegar
1 teaspoon celery seeds
1 teaspoon tarragon
½ teaspoon black pepper

Combine cucumbers and onions in a large glass, stainless steel, or ceramic bowl. Sprinkle with salt and let stand 3 hours. Then rinse under cold tap water and drain well.
Combine remaining ingredients. Add drained vegetables. Mix well. Pack into freezer containers and freeze. Defrost in refrigerator for 8 hours before serving.
Yield: 4 pints.

*No-Cook Refrigerator Pickles

6 cups thinly sliced cucumbers
1 cup thinly sliced onions
1 cup sliced mangoes (optional)
2 teaspoons pickling salt
1 teaspoon celery seeds
2 cups white sugar
1 cup white vinegar
3 cups water

Mix all ingredients together. Allow mixture to stand for a few hours. Put in jars and store in refrigerator.

These pickles will keep for 6 months in the refrigerator.

Yield: 2 quarts.

Pickled Fruits and Vegetables

Spiced Pickled Cabbage

4 quarts shredded red or green cabbage
½ cup pickling salt
1 quart white vinegar
1 cup sugar
1 tablespoon mustard seeds
4 teaspoons grated horseradish
1 teaspoon whole cloves
4 cinnamon sticks

Layer cabbage and salt in a large kettle or crock. Let stand overnight. The next day, drain cabbage, pressing out all juice. Rinse thoroughly and drain again. In a saucepan, combine vinegar, sugar, mustard seeds, and horseradish. Bring to a boil. Tie cloves and cinnamon in a cheesecloth spice bag and add to saucepan. Simmer for 15 minutes.

Pack cabbage into clean, hot pint jars and fill with vinegar mixture, leaving ½ inch headspace. Remove air bubbles by running a nonmetallic spatula down sides of jars. Seal, and process in a boiling-water bath canner for 20 minutes.

Yield: 4 pints.

Green Tomato Olives

About 100 small, green cherry tomatoes
Several sprigs fresh dill
3 tablespoons mixed pickling spices
1½ cups flaked pickling salt
2 cups vinegar
8 quarts hot water

Wash and dry tomatoes. Do not core. Place a layer of dill and half the pickling spices in a stone crock or a largemouth, 1-gallon glass jar. Top with all the tomatoes, then add another layer of dill and the remaining spices. In a saucepan, dissolve the salt in the vinegar and water and bring to a boil. Let cool, then pour over the tomatoes. Over the top place a small plate which has been weighted to keep all the tomatoes well covered by the brine. Any tomatoes not immersed will spoil and ruin the entire batch. Cover the jar with a cloth and keep in a cool place (60° to 70° F.) about 3 weeks. Each day skim any scum off the top of the liquid, rinse off the plate and add more brine as necessary to keep tomatoes immersed. When tomatoes are well-flavored and even in color, they are cured and ready to eat or can.

To can, drain the "olives" and prepare fresh hot brine by bringing ¾ cup salt, 1 cup vinegar and 4 quarts water to a boil, stirring to dissolve salt. Fill 12 pint or 6 quart canning jars with tomatoes and add a fresh sprig of dill, 1 peeled clove of garlic and 1 bay leaf to each jar. Pour hot brine in each jar to within ½ inch of top. Process pints and quarts 10 minutes in boiling-water bath. Serve as you would olives.

Yield: 12 pints or 6 quarts.

Adapted from *52 Great Green Tomato Recipes*.

Sweet Green Wheels

35 to 40 small green tomatoes, sliced ¼ inch thick
10 small onions, sliced
2 quarts water
½ cup pickling salt
3 cups water
1 cup cider vinegar
1 teaspoon whole cloves
2 cinnamon sticks
2 tablespoons mixed pickling spices
4 cups cider vinegar
3 cups honey

Layer tomatoes and onions in a large stainless steel or porcelain bowl. Mix 2 quarts water with salt, pour over vegetables, and soak overnight. In the morning, drain and rinse well in cold water.

Pour tomatoes and onions into a large stainless steel pot, and add 3 cups cold water and 1 cup vinegar. Simmer about 1 hour, or until light in color. Combine cloves, cinnamon, and pickling spices in a muslin spice bag. Place in a separate pot with remaining cider vinegar and honey. Boil for 10 minutes.

Fill clean, hot pint jars with tomato and onion mixture. Pour in syrup, leaving ½ inch headspace. Seal and process for 10 minutes in a boiling-water bath canner.

Yield: 10 pints.

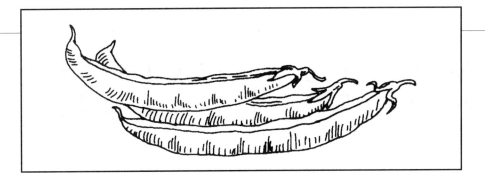

Beans Oriental

8 cups green beans (2 pounds)
4 cups white vinegar
1 cup water
2 tablespoons soy sauce
2 tablespoons cooking sherry
1½ cups sugar
1 tablespoon ground ginger or shredded
    ginger root
½ teaspoon cayenne pepper
4 bay leaves
4 cloves garlic

Wash beans and cut into 4-inch pieces. Combine vinegar, water, soy sauce, sherry, sugar, ginger, and cayenne in a medium-size saucepan. Bring to a boil. Place 1 bay leaf and 1 garlic clove in each clean, hot pint jar. Pack tightly with beans. Cover with hot syrup, leaving ½ inch headspace, and seal. Process in a boiling-water bath canner for 10 minutes.

Yield: 4 pints.

Pickled Beets

10 to 12 pounds beets
1 quart cider vinegar
⅔ cup sugar
1 cup water
2 tablespoons pickling salt

Cut tops and roots off flush with beet. Scrub thoroughly. Place beets on a rack in a large roaster. Cover and bake at 400° F. until tender, about 1 hour for medium-size beets. Meanwhile, preheat hot water and jars in canner.

In a saucepan, mix vinegar, sugar, water, and salt. Heat to boiling. When beets are tender, fill roaster with cold water. Slip skins off beets. Pack whole or cut in clean, hot pint jars. Add brine to cover. Leave ½ inch headspace. Process in a boiling-water bath canner for 10 minutes.

Yield: 7 pints.

Middle Eastern Cauliflower Pickles

These pickles turn a shocking pink. A perfect gift pickle.

3 heads cauliflower (4½ to 5 pounds)
3 cups white vinegar
6 cups water
2 tablespoons pickling salt
1 tablespoon cumin seeds
6 slices horseradish root
3 small beets, cooked and sliced

Wash cauliflower and cut into small flowerets. Steam over boiling water for 1 minute. Do not overcook. In a medium-size saucepan combine vinegar, water, salt, and cumin seeds. Bring to a boil and simmer for 5 minutes.

In the meantime, place 1 slice horseradish root and a couple of beet slices in each clean, hot pint jar. Pack tightly with cauliflower. Cover with hot brine, leaving ½ inch headspace. Seal. Process in a boiling-water bath canner for 15 minutes. Allow the jars to sit for at least a few days for full color to develop.

Yield: 6 pints.

*Sweet Pickled Pears or Peaches

To substitute peaches, dip briefly in hot water, then rub off fuzz with a towel. Stick each peach with 4 cloves instead of 3.

½ peck pears (6 to 7 pounds)
Cloves
2 pounds brown sugar
2 cups cider vinegar
1 ounce stick cinnamon

Wash pears. Pare only if skins are tough. Large pears may be quartered. Stick each pear with 3 cloves. Boil sugar, vinegar, and cinnamon for 20 minutes. Add pears, and cook in syrup only until tender when pricked with a fork. Fill hot, sterilized jars with fruit, add hot syrup, and seal.

To store the fruit in a crock instead of jars, fill with pears, cover with syrup, and place a plate on top to hold pears beneath syrup. Store in a cool, dry place, or refrigerate.

Yield: 3 to 4 quarts.

Watermelon Rind Pickles

8 cups watermelon rind (1 large
    watermelon)
½ cup pickling salt
2 quarts water
2 cups white vinegar
3 cups white or brown sugar
1 thinly sliced lemon
2 cinnamon sticks
1 teaspoon allspice berries
1 teaspoon whole cloves

Remove skin and pink from rind. Cut into 1-inch cubes. Soak overnight in a brine mixture of ½ cup salt and 2 quarts water. Drain and rinse. Drain again. Add more water to cover and simmer until tender. Drain.

Make a syrup of vinegar, sugar, lemon, and spices tied in a cheesecloth bag. Simmer for 5 minutes. Add rind and cook until it is clear. Pack into clean, hot pint jars and fill with syrup, leaving ½ inch headspace. Process in a boiling-water bath canner for 10 minutes.

Yield: 3 pints.

Spiced Apples

This recipe can be used with pears, too.

9 pounds hard, tart cooking apples
1 cup whole cloves (approximately)
2 pounds brown sugar
1 cup maple syrup
4 cups cider vinegar
1 cup white sugar
4 cups water
2 teaspoons pickling salt
8 cinnamon sticks

Wash, halve, and core apples, but do not peel. Stick 2 cloves in each piece. Combine remaining ingredients and bring to a boil. Place apples in spiced liquid and simmer for 5 minutes. Pack tightly into clean, hot jars. Cover with hot syrup, leaving ½ inch headspace. Seal. Process for 15 minutes in a boiling-water bath canner.

Wait 2 months before opening.

Yield: 12 pints.

Rhubarb-Raisin Relish

1 cup brown sugar
1 cup cider vinegar
1 cup water
½ teaspoon allspice
½ teaspoon cloves
1 stick cinnamon
½ teaspoon mustard seed
¼ teaspoon celery seed
1 cup onion, chopped
1½ cups fresh or thawed rhubarb, sliced
1 cup seedless raisins

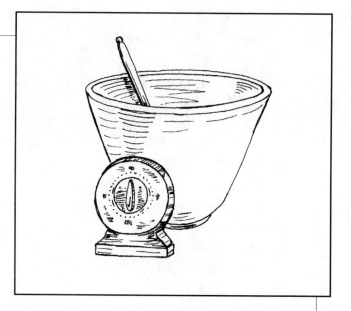

Combine first 8 ingredients in enamel kettle and boil 2 minutes. Add onions and rhubarb. Cover and cook slowly 30 minutes.

Rinse and drain raisins. Add them to rhubarb mixture and cook, uncovered, for 10 minutes. Stir well, pour into bowl, and refrigerate for immediate use or, while hot, seal in sterile glass jars and process 15 minutes in a boiling-water bath.

Makes 2 pints.

Adapted from *Great Rhubarb Recipes.*

Corn Relish

8 cups raw corn cut from the cob
3 cups chopped onions
½ cup chopped green pepper
½ cup chopped sweet red pepper
¾ cup packed brown sugar
½ cup white corn syrup
7 teaspoons pickling salt
1 tablespoon dry mustard
3 cups cider vinegar

Mix all ingredients thoroughly. Cover and boil for 15 minutes, stirring often. Pour into clean, hot pint jars, leaving ½ inch headspace. Seal. Process in a boiling-water bath canner for 15 minutes.

Yield: 4 to 5 pints.

Grand Scale Zucchini Relish

10 cups minced zucchini
1 cup pickling salt
5 cups minced onion
1 cup diced celery
3 green peppers, diced
2 sweet red peppers, diced
2 teaspoons turmeric
1 tablespoon dry mustard
3 tablespoons celery seeds
6 cups sugar
5 cups white vinegar
3 tablespoons cornstarch

Combine zucchini with salt and other vegetables. Allow to stand overnight. Drain. Rinse thoroughly and drain again in a colander. Force out as much liquid as possible.

In a large enamel pot, combine remaining ingredients; add the vegetables and bring to a rolling boil. Reduce heat and boil gently for 20 minutes. Ladle relish into clean, hot pint jars, leaving ½ inch headspace, and seal. Process in a boiling-water bath canner for 15 minutes.

Yield: 8 pints.

Connie's Pear Chutney

10 cups (about 5 pounds) sliced, firm,
    ripe pears
½ cup finely chopped green pepper
1½ cups seedless raisins
4 cups sugar
1 cup chopped crystallized ginger
3 cups cider vinegar
½ teaspoon pickling salt
½ teaspoon allspice berries
½ teaspoon whole cloves
3 cinnamon sticks, 2 inches long

Place pears and next 6 ingredients in a saucepan. Tie allspice and cloves in a cheesecloth bag and add along with cinnamon. Cook slowly until pears are tender and mixture thick, about 1 hour.

Remove spices. Ladle into clean, hot half-pint jars, leaving ½ inch headspace. Seal. Process for 10 minutes in a boiling-water bath canner.

Yield: 10 half-pints.

Tomato Chutney

6 pounds ripe medium-size tomatoes
    (about 24)
6 pounds tart green apples (about 12
    medium-size)
2 pounds onions (about 6 medium-size)
½ pound red peppers (about 3)
½ pound sweet green peppers (about 3)
1 cup minced celery
5 cups cider or malt vinegar
2½ cups sugar
4 tablespoons pickling salt
1 pound sultana-type raisins

Peel and chop tomatoes, apples, and onions. Chop peppers. Combine with the celery, vinegar, sugar, and salt in a large kettle.

Boil rapidly, stirring constantly, until mixture is clear and slightly thick. Add raisins and boil 20 to 30 minutes more. Keep stirring to avoid scorching. When sauce is reduced to 7 pints, put into clean, hot pint jars and seal. Process in a boiling-water bath canner for 15 minutes.

Yield: 7 pints.

Honey French Dressing

½ cup olive oil or vegetable oil
2 tablespoons cider vinegar
1 tablespoon honey
2 teaspoons catsup
1 small clove garlic, minced
1 teaspoon soy sauce
¼ teaspoon salt
¼ teaspoon paprika
Dash cayenne pepper

Combine all of the ingredients in a jar and shake well until blended.
Store in the refrigerator.

Makes about ⅔ cup of dressing.

Adapted from Cooking with Honey.

Dressings and Sauces

Plum Sauce for Chinese Dishes

Try this sauce with homemade egg rolls or — luxuriously — on pancakes or waffles.

2½ cups fresh fruit (plums, apricots, peaches, or apples)
½ cup water
2 tablespoons cider vinegar
2 tablespoons honey
⅛ tablespoon salt
1 tablespoon soy sauce
1 small clove garlic, minced
Pinch ginger (optional)
Dash Tabasco sauce (optional)

Skin and chop the fruit. Combine all of the ingredients in a saucepan and slowly bring to a boil. Simmer uncovered until all the fruit is tender but not too soft. Cool before serving.

Makes 4 servings.

Adapted from Cooking with Honey.

Honey Fruit Salad Dressing

4 ounces cream cheese
2 tablespoons honey
¼ cup yogurt
2 tablespoons heavy cream
2 tablespoons lemon juice

Mash the cream cheese until soft. Add the honey, yogurt, and cream. Cream until smooth. Add the lemon juice.

Makes 1 cup.

Adapted from Cooking with Honey.

Herb Dip

This flavorful dip is perfect for a platter of fresh vegetables cut into bite-size pieces (crudités). It could be made entirely with cottage cheese, or, for a more tangy flavor, yogurt could be substituted for the sour cream.

1 cup cottage cheese

½ cup sour cream

2 tablespoons minced onion

2 tablespoons wheat germ

2 teaspoons fresh thyme, or ¼ teaspoon
   dried thyme

2 tablespoons chopped fresh parsley

4 drops Tabasco sauce

¼ teaspoon oregano

Freshly ground pepper to taste

Mix all the ingredients in a bowl. Then transfer to a small serving bowl, garnish with fresh parsley or thyme, and surround with crisp fresh vegetables, such as cucumber spears, carrot circles, broccoli flowers, and mushroom slices.

Makes 1 ½ cups.

Adapted from *Salt-Free Herb Cookery.*

Thousand Island Dressing

2 medium green tomatoes

1 cup mayonnaise or salad dressing

1 tablespoon green pepper, chopped

1 tablespoon sweet red pepper, chopped

¼ teaspoon paprika

2 tablespoons chopped olives

Peel green tomatoes and scoop seeds and pulp from centers. Discard pulp and finely chop outer shells. Combine with remaining ingredients and mix well.

Makes about 2 cups dressing.

Will keep a week or two in the refrigerator.

Adapted from *52 Great Green Tomato Recipes.*

Except as noted, material in t his chapter has been excerpted and adapted from Favorite Pickles & Relishes, *Storey/Garden Way Publishing Country Wisdom Bulletin #A-91*

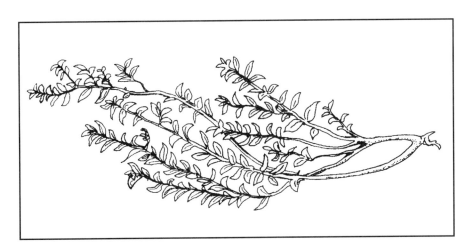

CHAPTER 3

Bottled Gifts

Making Your Own Wine

Wine is probably the most ancient and widespread alcoholic drink. It has been around several thousand years, as the literature of both the ancient Greeks and Hebrews tells us. Today, alcohol is available as wines, beers, and distilled spirits. But wine is most popular with home brewers.

Wine is the easiest alcohol to make. It does not require fastidious temperature control or a still. You can make fine wines from grapes or other fruits, or from vegetables, grains, or flowers.

This chapter will take the mystery out of making wine. We teach you the language and explain ingredients and equipment. We offer reliable, delicious recipes, and we help you cure or prevent common problems. So, enjoy!

Vintners' Language

As with any specialty, winemaking has a language all its own. Some terms:

Champagning: The process of trapping carbonation into a still wine with a second, sealed ferment.

Cider: Low-alcohol (6 to 9 percent) wine made from apples. Sometimes made sparkling, usually made still.

Fining: The removal of small-particle cloudiness from a wine.

Maderize: To cook a wine until it is like a Madeira. Wines stored at too high a temperature often will be said to be maderized.

Must: The dense liquid from which a wine begins. The point at which must starts being wine is around SG (specific gravity) 1.030, or the point at which 60 percent of the sugar is converted into alcohol to give an alcoholic content of at least 7 percent.

BOTTLED GIFTS 35

Pearl: The carbon dioxide bubbles in a very slightly fermenting wine. Some wines, designed for a texture between champagne and still wine, are bottled when there is still a slight pearl in them.

Perry: Cider made from pears. See cider.

Plonk: A corruption of the French blanc, often used to denote a common white wine of French origin.

Rack: To siphon wine from one vessel to another.

Specific gravity: The density of a liquid as a fraction of the weight of water. A wine must with a lot of sugar in it will weigh between 8 percent and 12 percent more than water, hence will have a specific gravity (SG) of between 1.080 and 1.120. When these musts ferment out to the point where no sugar is left, they will give wines that weigh between 0.7 percent and 1.2 percent less than water (alcohol being lighter than water). The more alcoholic a finished dry wine is, the lower its SG.

Vinify: Literally, "to turn to wine."

Essential Equipment

These are the few items you will need to get started in home winemaking.

Air locks: These let carbon dioxide gas out of the carboy and prevent air from getting in. Buy one for each carboy.

Carboys: Large glass vessels used as secondary fermenters. Carboys hold 5 gallons of liquid. You need an extra empty carboy to rack wine into, so buy 1 more carboy than you plan to make batches of wine.

Funnel: Buy a large one.

Hose and J-tube: For siphoning and keeping the siphon level above the dead yeast in the bottom of the vessel.

Hydrometer set: Includes a hydrometer to measure the sugar content in the must and a tall tube.

Nylon bag: Select a fine-mesh or medium-mesh bag, measuring 2 feet by 2 feet. It is used with a mallet to make a homemade juice extractor.

Plastic sheet: To cover the vat.

Spoon: A long-handled wooden spoon works best; but a plastic one is acceptable. Used for stirring the must.

Strainer: Any large kitchen sieve will do.

String: Take a string that is 4 inches less than the circumference of your vat, and tie the ends to a 3-inch rubber band. Then you have an elastic tightener to hold the sheet on the vat.

Titration kit: Measures acidity of the must.

Vat: You will need a large vessel, or vat, for the initial fermenting stage. I am partial to a 17-gallon garbage pail.

Helpful but Not Essential Items

Corker: For inserting corks in bottles.

Crown capper: Needed if you intend to make sparkling wines or ciders.

Crusher: Necessary for any large-scale operation using fresh fruit. It is not necessary for 10- or 20-gallon batches. Crushers can be rented, but if you go to press frequently you may want to own one.

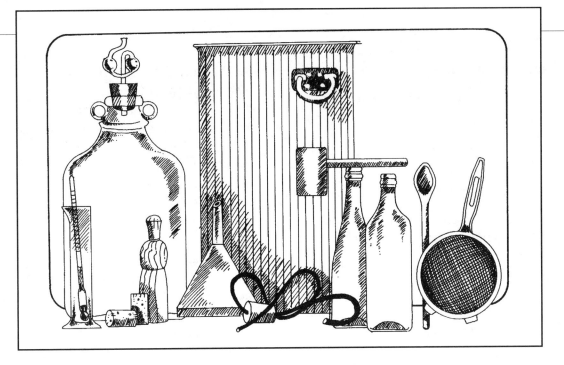

De-stemmer: For taking stems off fresh grapes. A large wooden spaghetti server makes an adequate substitute.

Filter and pump: These are used as a last-ditch method of clarification. I have used one once in 250 batches of wine.

Gallon jugs: These are useful in the stage between carboy and bottle. Sometimes restaurants give them away.

Vinometer: Measures alcohol in wines that are fermented out and dry; it is not useful for wines with residual sugar.

Wine press: Device for pressing fruit either before or at the end of the first fermentation in the vat. It is necessary if you are making over 100 gallons a year of fresh grape or fresh fruit wine.

Ingredients

These are the ingredients you will need, in addition to fruit, to make wine at home.

Essential Ingredients — Long Shelf-Lives

Acid blend: Raises acidity level of low-acid must and flabby finished wine.

Campden Tablets: Disinfects fresh must and wines during racking.

Disinfectant: Solution of water and potassium metabisulfite crystals, kept in gallon jug. Essential for cleanliness.

Grape tannin powder: Enhances the flavor and gutsiness of cider, perry, and wines made from concentrates.

Essential — but Perishable — Ingredients

Pectic enzymes: Removes the pectic haze from fruit wines and is put into the must just before yeast; 3-month shelf life.

Yeast culture, liquid or powdered: Essential to fermentation, the yeast organisms turn sugar to alcohol. Unopened it has a one-year shelf life.

Optional Ingredients

Finings: A powder used to remove microscopic particles that cloud wine.

Glycerine: Adds finish to table wines.

Oak chips: For adding barrel taste, especially to red wines.

Pure unflavored grain or grape alcohol: Fortifies port, sherry, and Madeira.

Sorbic acid (potassium sorbate): Stabilizes the wine before bottling.

Vitamin C tablets, 250 mg: Protects white wines from oxidation.

Basic Techniques of Winemaking

There are only four requirements for successful winemaking.

- The weight or sugar content should be enough to read 1.060 to 1.080 on a hydrometer scale. (All hydrometer readings in this book are given in the form of specific gravity (SG), that is, a fraction of the weight of water.)

- The acidity of your must should measure .55 to .80 percent to prevent early deterioration. Obtain this reading with your titration kit.

- Proper temperatures must be maintained. During the first 10 days of fermentation, temperature of the must should measure at a maximum of 76° F. for red wines and 70° F. for fruit wines and white wines. The temperature of the must should never dip below 55° F. Remember that fermenting must generates quite a bit of heat.

- Absolute cleanliness. This means keeping air out of contact with fermenting juice and wine, and meticulous sterilization of all equipment before and after use. To sterilize equipment, use a sulfite solution made from crystals available from your wine-supply dealer.

Given these things, you need only a live yeast culture, some primitive equipment, and some patience in order to make good wine. There is nothing complicated or even difficult about the process.

There are eight stages of winemaking, and we will take you through the first seven: preparation, primary fermentation, secondary fermentation, aging in the carboy, fining (an optional stage), finishing and bottling, and cellaring. Drinking the wine is the final stage, and you are on your own for that.

The processes we describe take days, weeks, and months. There is time to master each step as you go along. You will make your wine one stage at a time, beginning with the preparations.

Preparing the Equipment

Careful sterilization of all gear with a sulfite solution is essential. Here are a few rules for cleaning equipment.

- Never use detergent; use only a chlorine solution for stains and a sulfite solution, mixed with a gallon of warm water and a packet of crystals from a winemakers' supply store.

- Rinse glassware inside with warm water, then drain, then rinse with sulfite solution. If the glassware is going to be stored, it should be stoppered with a small amount of solution in it (⅛ inch on the bottom). Bottles about to be used immediately may be rinsed again with water, but it is not necessary.

- Sterilize corks and screw caps by a 60-second total immersion in sulfite solution; do not boil corks.

- If fruit pulp sticks to your gear, use a plastic abrasive pad and hot water to remove it.

- When putting away your primary fermenters for a while, rinse with sulfite solution, cover with a plastic sheet, and secure with a tight string.

Starting the Yeast Culture

For making more than 3 gallons of wine, you will need to mix yeast culture with a starter solution. For smaller quantities, the yeast may be added directly to the must from vial or packet.

Two or three days before the must is to be crushed or put together, make up the following recipe.

Wine Starter

3 ounces frozen orange juice concentrate
24 ounces water
6 ounces sugar
2 rounded teaspoons of ordinary yeast nutrient

Put the frozen orange juice, water, and sugar into a 2-quart saucepan, and bring the mix to a boil. Remove it from the heat, add the nutrient, and cover the pot until the mix cools to room temperature.

Transfer the starter mix to a sterilized 1-gallon jug, add the yeast culture, and stopper the jug with an air lock. After 24 to 36 hours, "islands" of active yeast should appear on the surface of the liquid. Give the jug a swirl every 6 to 8 hours. When the solution gets to an active ferment (much CO_2 is expelled through the air lock when you swirl), it is ready to add to the must.

Always prestart your yeast for any batch of wine 3 gallons or more. The recipe given above will handle any quantity of wine from 3 to 12 gallons; for larger quantities you will want to double, triple or quadruple the recipe.

Preparing the Fruit

After you have removed all the stems and leaves from your washed fruit, it is ready for crushing. You can use a commercially available crusher or improvise with a large plastic container and wooden mallet. With white grapes, as well as with many tree fruits, press out the vegetable matter in a press, so the must consists of nothing but juice. With red grapes, ferment first for 5 to 10 days and then press. If you are making no more than 35 or 40 gallons a year, you can use a medium-mesh or fine-mesh nylon bag to get the effect of a pressing. Just crush your fruit in the bag, then squeeze the juice out.

Add hot water and other ingredients to the crushed fruit, and you have a must, or a liquid nearly ready to ferment. Add to the must some Campden Tablets to keep it free of debilitating organisms.

Testing the Must

First, test the must with a hydrometer. If the must weight is between 1.080 and

Winemaking: Step by Step

1. Wash the fruits, remove all stems and leaves. Then crush the fruit.

2. Add crushed Campden Tablets.

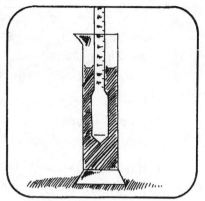

3. Test the must with a hydrometer and titration kit.

4. Add the yeast starter.

5. Cover the must tightly with a plastic sheet and secure it with a string.

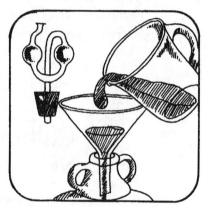

6. When the weight of the must reaches SG 1.025 to 1.030, transfer the must to a carboy and fit the top with an air lock.

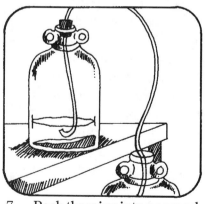

7. Rack the wine into a secondary fermenter.

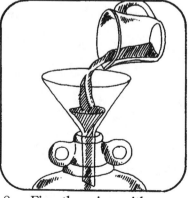

8. Fine the wine with a special gelatin solution and rack again.

9. Bottle the wine.

1.095, don't tinker. If it is below 1.080, add sugar; above 1.095, cut the must somewhat with water, unless you want a very sweet or alcoholic wine. Temperature has a large effect on specific gravity readings, and hydrometers are calibrated to be accurate when the must is at 60° or 68° F.

Next, test for acidity with a titration kit. If it is a red must and the acidity is .65 percent, or a white must and the acidity is .75 percent, you will be happy indeed. If acidity is too low, add an acid blend (citric, malic, or tartaric). With shipped California grapes, the natural acidity will be too low. If it's too high (as with Eastern grapes) cut the must somewhat with a sugar and water solution of weight 1.090, or with a dilute low-acidity must made from a hot-climate concentrate (available from wine supply stores).

You can get to this stage more quickly and easily by using a grape concentrate from a winemakers' supply store or by using grape juice shipped to a juicer in your nearest urban area. You should not be put off by previous unhappy experiences with concentrates. In the last few years, Wine-Art Ltd. of Toronto, a marketer of home wine products, has been selling concentrates from Australia that make wines indistinguishable from those made with fresh grapes.

Adding the Yeast Culture

Last add the yeast culture, now fermenting in the starter solution.

Primary Fermentation

After you have adjusted weight and acidity, and added a yeast culture, the vat in which this first (primary) fermentation goes on should be covered with a tight-fitting plastic sheet, fastened with string. Once a vigorous, rolling ferment is started (24 to 48 hours), stir the must and push down the "cap" (the vegetable crust that will form on the top) twice a day. Use a well-sterilized wooden spoon.

Weigh the must every day after the third day, to see how rapidly the fermentation is going. A loss of .007 to .015 per day is good; more than that indicates that the must should be moved to a cooler place.

Test the must frequently with your best piece of winemaker's test equipment — your nose. The smell of a fermenting must is pervasive, sometimes throughout the house. If there is an aroma in addition to those of fruit and CO_2 coming from the wine, do not be disturbed unless that aroma has a strong sulfur or vinegar cast to it. In that case, turn to our troubleshooting section, pages 46 to 48.

When the weight reaches 1.025 to 1.030, transfer the must to disinfected glass carboys with a siphon and J-tube. If you are making a red wine, press out the residual fruit in the fermenting vat. (Again, the nylon bag is a useful alternative to a press.) Stopper the carboys with air locks filled with sulfite solution to permit CO_2 to escape and prevent air contact with the wine. Leave the wine in the primary fermenter for 5 to 10 days.

Secondary Fermentation

For the secondary fermentation, rack the wine into freshly disinfected carboys. To rack wine from a primary to secondary fermenter, place the vessel with the wine in it on a table at least 30 inches high. Put the sterilized carboy or jug on the floor. Take a 5- or 6-foot length of clear tubing with a J-tube on the end, and place the J-tube into the wine, on the bottom of the vessel. Apply suction on the plastic hose to fill it; put the discharge end quickly into the vessel you are filling. When the wine is completely transferred, rinse and sterilize the used vessel and the plastic tubing. Change the disinfectant in the air locks.

Check the weight of your wine at this point, too. A weight of 1.005 to 1.010 will be average, though a wine with a vigorous yeast in it may well be below 1.000. As long as the wine is sending even the occasional bubble up through the air lock, it is actively fermenting.

Measure specific gravity with a hydrometer. Some hydrometers are calibrated to read accurately at 60° F., others at 68° F. Make sure you are reading your hydrometer at the proper temperature.

To read a hydrometer, ignore the way the liquid curves against the stem and tube because of surface tension, and take the reading from the level portion of the liquid.

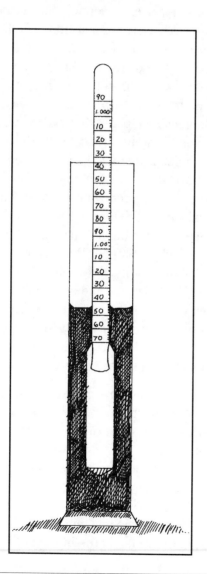

To rack the wine to a secondary fermenter, use a plastic J-tube and siphon the wine from the first carboy to the second. Keep the original carboy 30 inches higher than the fresh carboy. Be sure that the end of the tube is completely submerged in the wine. This prevents the wine from coming in contact with air.

Aging

Rack your wine again in another 6 to 12 weeks, adding 1 crushed Campden Tablet per gallon. I prefer a 6-week interval, especially with fruit wines. Three months after the second racking, you should rack again, adding more Campden Tablets. After this, rack every 6 months.

Change the disinfectant in the air locks every 3 months. SO_2 in solution is highly volatile, and fruit flies, which tend to carry vinegar bacteria on them, are massively persistent. Fresh disinfectant in the air lock is the best way to keep them out.

Fining

At the sixth month (perhaps even as soon as the sixth week with Cluett's Plonk, or the third month with some of the lower acidity wines from concentrate), you may want to fine your white wines.

Fining, the removal of small-particle cloudiness from a wine, was once done with bull's blood or egg white. Far better to use a gelatin-based fining sold under several brand names. The most commonly used brand is Sparkalloid.

The special gelatin, in hot solution, is poured into a carboy of wine and coagulates around small particles that cloud the wine, carrying them to the bottom of the carboy. After it has done its work (1 to 28 days), you can rack the clear wine off the fined gunk that has settled to the bottom. The wine can then be stabilized (by adding ¾ teaspoon of sorbic acid per gallon) and put into jugs or bottles, or simply left in the carboy to age further.

Finishing

Between the seventh and the twelfth month you will bottle most white wines, some reds, and most other fruit wines. Make sure that there is no threat of renewed fermentation in the wine; if that occurs after the wine is bottled, you will get some nasty explosions in your cellar.

Preventing renewed fermentation can be done in either of two ways. One way is to keep the wine under an air lock until it reaches a weight between .993 (for a starting weight of 1.080) and .990 (for a starting weight of 1.100), and not bottle before. This can involve an indefinite wait. Fermentation can stick at weights like .996 or .998, which indicate residual sugar in the wine and probably residual live yeast. Wines can sit for 18 and 24 months at .998, then suddenly reignite after a change in the weather. It seems best to stabilize the wine by adding ¾ teaspoon of sorbic acid

(potassium sorbate) per gallon, whatever the weight of a wine when bottling.

There is an alternative to bottling: aging the wine in a gallon jug between carboy and bottle. With wines for which I have further plans, such as champagning, I use an air lock on the jug; other wines get ¾ teaspoon of sorbic acid and a screw cap. Using the gallon jug has many advantages. With jug wines like Cluett's Plonk, it is far preferable to have 4 wide-mouth, stoppered, 1-liter carafes that can be kept in the refrigerator. The wine will last nicely for 5 to 6 weeks. A further advantage is that the gallon jug leaves you flexibility for blending wines, especially reds. Some of your wines will be too dark, some too light, some too tannic, some too smooth (a forecast of short life). Such wines, so long as they do not taste outright bad, will often benefit from being blended with wines of opposite character. I keep a few gallon jugs of elderberry-enriched Petite Syrah on hand to give backbone and color to the pale, pale California Carignane of which I make a carboy or so each year.

Oaking

At this point (seventh month) you will probably want to add a packet of oak chips (available from your wine supply dealer) to your better reds for about a month. This process adds oak tannin and barrel flavor to the wine and is generally beneficial. To remove the chips, rack the wine again.

After the oaking, which you may want to do a second time on some wines, taste the wine for finish, or ability to hang on the palate. First, swirl an inch of wine around in a large wine glass. If it leaves glycerine streaks down the side of the glass (so-called legs), you have a good sign. Second, put the wine into your mouth, squeeze it

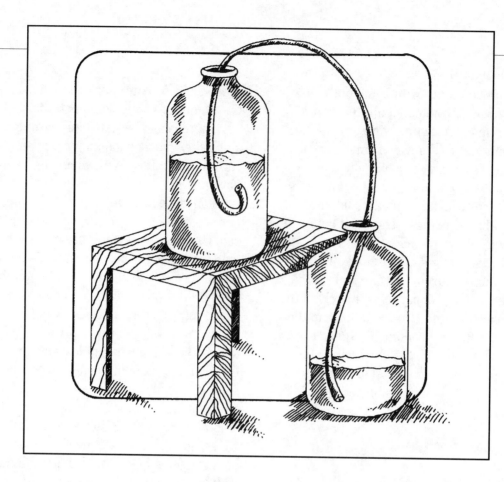

into the corners back of your teeth and under your tongue, and then swallow. If the flavor of the wine and its intensity last after swallowing, then you have a second good sign. If the wine throws no or few legs, or if it quits quickly after being swallowed, then add 4 ounces of glycerine to the carboy and repeat the two tests about 8 weeks later, adding more glycerine if the wine is still unleggy or faint on the palate. Some time around the eighteenth month, stabilize and bottle your better reds.

Bottling

I always bottle and cork my better wines. Cork breathes slightly and allows the very slow process of oxidation that facilitates the aging of wine. The better the wine, the more worthy it is of being corked.

Do not use recycled corks. Use new, waxed corks from a reliable supplier. Your cork should be at least 1¼ inches long, with a diameter slightly larger than that of the mouth of the bottle.

Before bottling, prepare the corks. Place them in water that just has been boiled (never boil the corks), cover the vessel, and leave them for 5 minutes. Then place them in a sulfite solution, pushing them down to cover them fully with sulfite. Then they are ready to use, and you can siphon your wine into a sterilized bottle. Recycled glass — not plastic — bottles are okay, but make sure that they have been completely cleaned and rinsed with sulfite solution.

Many devices are available for driving home corks — from $2 wooden gadgets to $150 production-line devices. My own preference is the San-Bri hand corker from France, which retails for about $10 and is both quick and reliable. This corker has a metal collar for squeezing the cork and a piston for driving it home.

When you cork the wine, do not countersink the cork; keep it level with or slightly above the very top of the bottle opening. One further suggestion: If you use a hand corker of any kind, put the filled bottles into divided wine cases before corking them; this prevents the bottles from spontaneously overturning, spilling wine or breaking glassware.

As for putting a plastic or metal seal over the top and neck of the bottle, I don't. The capsule is strictly a decoration, and it impedes the breathing of the cork.

Cellaring

After bottling, you are usually in for a wait of 6 months or more, possibly much more. Periodic checking is the key to timing the consumption of the wine at its peak point. Unless a wine is hideously astringent (in which case an annual check is enough), opening a new bottle every 6 months will be enough to keep you abreast of progress. Patience can be a great healer of the problems of a wine. Several friends have produced wines they pronounced "undrinkable" at an early stage, only to see the wines turn highly drinkable 3 to 5 years later. Don't give up too soon. Much is made of "correct" storage, and some of the myths are down-right silly. There are, however, four basic rules for cellaring that have the force of sacred writ.

- Store wine away from light, especially direct sunlight or fluorescent fixtures; these kinds of light maderize wine, or

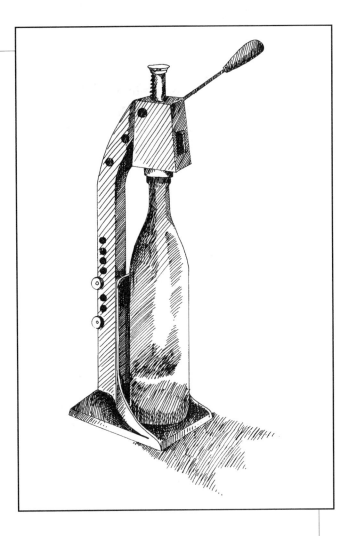

make it go off in flavor.

- Store corked wines on their sides. If they are stored upright, the corks dry out, and air gets to the wine, ruining it.

- Wine storage temperature should never go over 75° F., except for brief spans of time. At 75° F., wine begins to oxidize.

- Temperature in a wine storage area should be as steady as possible; changes should be gradual. A 68° to 73° F. storage area is far preferable to one whose range is 45 to 65° F., even though the first one approaches the dangerous 75° F. figure. Rises in temperature force wine through the cork; drops cause air to be sucked back in. The greater the changes in temperature a wine suffers, the greater its premature aging from over-breathing.

Follow these guidelines, and your cellar (or closet) will never ruin a well-made bottle of wine.

The rate of maturation, especially in red wines, will vary enormously with the style of vinification. You can vinify with the stems left on the grapes and get much more tannin and acidity into your wine; this will mean early harshness but longer life. Similarly, the more complete your pressing of the grapes, the more tannin, acid, and coloring matter will go into the wine. To vinify a red wine lighter, press sooner (but leave the wine in vat until its weight reaches 1.030), and press more lightly. Filtration, too, will make a lighter, faster-maturing wine.

Troubleshooting

Because each of us has a distinct style of going about things, we each will evolve a distinctive set of winemaking problems — and solutions for them. There are, however, certain problems that plague about 95 percent of the winemaking population. What follows is a handy guide to the Universal Ills of Winekind, ordered by their probable place in the life of the wine.

1. Stuck starter: the yeast will not ignite. The cause: either the starter was too cool or the yeast too old. The cure: move the bottle atop the refrigerator or get new yeast. Next time keep the starter at a temperature of 68° to 72° F., and deal only with a first-class supplier.

2. Stuck ferment in the primary fermenter (first week to 10 days) has four probable causes.

    •   If the must or wine gets too hot (above 76° F.), the heat will kill the yeast. The cure: move to a cooler place; add freshly started yeast culture. Prevent it next time by watching the temperature carefully.

    •   If the must is too cool (under 58° F.), the yeast will not ignite. The cure: move the must to a warmer place. Watch the temperature.

    •   If the must is too heavy (SG 1.115 or more), the sugar will inhibit fermentation. The cure: cut the must with water and acid blend. To prevent it, add the sugar in stages, rather than at the beginning. (I presume in this case you want a wine that is alcoholic or sweet or both.)

    •   If there is not enough nutrient for the yeast, fermentation is inhibited. This is especially likely with blueberry, pear, and peach must. The cure: add nutrient and fresh yeast culture.

3. Stuck ferment in the secondary fermenter (carboy) can be caused by all of the above. Sometimes the wine sticks (often at SG 1.012) for causes that are utterly mysterious. The cure: add "supernutrient," a magnesium and vitamin B mix that gives you a stronger kick than the ordinary ammonia and uric acid nutrient. If

that fails, add fresh yeast culture. If that fails, wait for the wine to clear, and add it in a 1 to 5 ratio to other wines that are in a healthy secondary fermentation. Otherwise, resign yourself to having made a sweet wine. Before you bottle this wine, stabilize.

4. Hydrogen sulfide (rotten egg aroma) is a special threat to low-acid wines, notably Cluett's Plonk and any wine made from vinifera grapes that have been shipped a long distance. It smells like rotten eggs, and it usually occurs in the second to fourth week of the wine's life — although I have had it happen in hot weather during the fifth day. The cause is dead yeast and dead fruit pulp working together in low-acid wine. The cure: pour the wine (do not siphon) into a fresh carboy with 1 Campden Tablet per gallon. Use a funnel and make sure the wine is well aerated. This is the only exception to the general rule to keep air out of wine. The prevention is to rack more often and watch acidity levels.

5. Mycoderma appear as grey islands of organisms on the wine; they are caused by poor sanitation. The cure: immediately strain the wine through fine cotton mesh and add 2 Campden Tablets per gallon. Once mycoderma have covered the entire surface of the wine, however, the wine must be thrown out. Prevent this by keeping your equipment sterilized and keeping air out of your wine.

6. Vinegar smell and taste is caused by poor sanitation. There is no cure, the

Day-to-Day Summary

Day 1   Start your yeast culture.

Day 3   Crush and de-stem the fruit. Add Campden Tablets. Weigh, test for acidity, adjust for sugar and acid balance. Press (white and most fruit wines), add yeast to the must in premixed starter.

Day 4 or 5   Break up the cap and stir. Do this daily thereafter until wine reaches a specific gravity of 1.030.

Day 10   (Or when the wine reaches a specific gravity of 1.030.) Press out the grapes in red wines. Rack all wines into carboys and stopper with air locks and sulfite.

Day 25   Rack into fresh carboys. Add Campden Tablets.

Month 3   Rack again, and again 3 months later, and every 6 months thereafter.

Month 7   (Or sooner.) Fine whites. Stabilize and bottle most whites, some reds. Red wines may be oaked.

Month 8   Check reds for finish. Add glycerine if needed.

Month 12   White wine bottled in month 7 is probably drinkable. Beaujolais from France and other light reds may also be ready to serve.

Month 18   Bottle better reds. Wait minimum of 6 months to drink them.

Month 24 to year 40   Wines become drinkable and reach their age limits.

wine is lost. Next time, keep equipment sterilized and keep air out of your wine.

7. When browning occurs in white wines there is no real cure, but the browning can be halted by adjusting the acid balance, adding ascorbic acid (250 mg/gallon), and keeping air out. Prevent browning by avoiding over-ripe fruit and contact between wine and air.

8. Stuck fining happens when the wine is too warm or too low in acid. The cure: add 1 tablespoon of acid blend to the carboy, decrease the temperature by 5° F. If this fails, rent a filter and pump from your friendly local supply house and use them. The next time, fine your wine at proper temperature (65° F. and under) and acidity (.06 or more).

9. Explosion or spontaneous degorgement is caused by residual sugar and live yeast in the wine when bottled. The cure: unbottle all remaining wine of that batch to a carboy, add potassium sorbate, and rebottle. Prevent this by reading the hydrometer carefully and stabilizing the wine before bottling.

10. Bottle odor when wine is opened has two causes.

    • A sulfur odor means there was too much sulfite in the bottle when it was filled. The cure: decant the wine an hour before drinking; leave the decanter unstoppered. The SO_2 will evaporate. Next time, when you bottle your wine, rinse the bottles with water after sterilizing them; or keep them upside down after sterilizing.

    • A mildew odor indicates a rotten cork or mildewed fruit. There is no cure; but open two or three bottles from the same batch to see if all are affected. If all the bottles have a mildew taste in the wine, scrap the batch. If only some bottles have mildew in the wine, recork the sound bottles. Prevent this problem with strict attention to sanitation. Also, remove suspect fruit before you crush.

11. Undue harshness is caused by too much acidity, tannin, youth, all three, or any two thereof. The cure: patience, and blending with wine of opposite character. Give the wine at least a few months before blending. Prevent this by using the best suppliers you can find for your fruits and concentrates.

Recipes

In the best of all possible worlds, we would have 135 pages for recipes and would cover everything from apricots to zucchini. Alas, we have had to be selective. The recipes were selected to cover cider, still wines, and champagne; the major kinds of materials (grape, other fruit, grain, and flower); and the tree and vine fruits most likely to come into the hands of home winemakers. If you are to use material not specifically covered here (rice, for example), use the recipe in our group that is closest to your material. In the case of rice, use the recipe for wheat.

By the way, we do not offer a specific recipe for grape wines. They have been covered both in the main text and in the Universal Recipe on page 56.

Once a recipe works reasonably well for you, you might try variations. For example, you can make a wine taste drier by adding a rounded teaspoon of acid blend per gallon. This does not, in fact, make the wine any drier (that is, lacking in sugar); it simply makes it more tart. You can make a wine sweet by starting with a SG of 1.115, or by stopping fermentation with sorbic acid at SG 1.002 to 1.005. You can give a wine longer life by adding extra tannin to the must before the yeast culture is added, or by the addition of stem, pip, or freeze-dried whole grapes. You can give a wine more alcohol by adding extra sugar to the must, preferably in stages after fermentation has begun.

The recipes do not specify the amount of yeast needed. Here is the rule. If you are making 3 gallons or less, simply add 1 packet or 1 vial of wine yeast culture to your must, when the must cools to 70° F. or less. If you are making over 3 gallons, start your yeast in the way described on page 39, then add it to the cooled must.

Where fruit concentrates are called for, I have not specified the exact amounts for some of the other ingredients. You will find instructions on the concentrate labels.

We will not repeat our injunctions about keeping everything absolutely sterile. In addition, it is a good protection to add a crushed Campden Tablet for each gallon of must at the beginning of fermentation, and an additional crushed Campden Tablet every second racking. When dealing with concentrates of juices, always ask the supplier about the need for Campden Tablets.

Cluett's Plonk

This makes an all-purpose dry white wine, ready to drink in 6 to 10 weeks.

1 unit (100 ounces) apricot concentrate
1 unit non-Labrusca white grape
    concentrate
Corn sugar (75 percent of what is called
    for on concentrate labels)
Grape tannin (as per labels)
Yeast nutrient (as per labels)
Acid blend (1½ ounces less than
    combined total on labels)
Warm water (as per labels)
Yeast culture
Pectic enzyme (as per labels)

Mix all the ingredients except the yeast and pectic enzyme in a 17-gallon plastic vat. The water temperature should be 105° to 110° F. Cover the vat with a plastic sheet secured with a string. Put the vat in a place that is room temperature (65° to 75° F.). Wait 24 hours, then measure the specific gravity and adjust to 1.080. Add water if the SG is too high; add sugar if it is too low. Measure acidity, and adjust to .55 to .60 percent by adding acid blend or water. If you add water, add sugar also to bring SG to 1.080. When the acid and SG levels are satisfactory, add the yeast culture and pectic enzyme.

Rack into carboys 5 days after fermentation starts; rack again in 10 days. This wine, with its high pulp content and low acidity, is very vulnerable to hydrogen sulfide and must be racked often. That's bad news, but one does not get a ready wine this quickly without paying a price.

This recipe makes two 5-gallon carboys or 50 bottles — almost a month's drinking.

Flower Wine

With honeysuckle and clover, some winemakers like to stabilize the wine with sorbic acid, then add sugar to SG 1.005 or 1.010 before bottling.

2 quarts flowers (dandelion heads, clover
    blossoms, or honeysuckle blossoms)
¼ pound raisins, chopped
Juice and peel of 2 oranges
Juice and peel of 2 lemons
3 pounds sugar
1 ounce acid blend
¼ teaspoon grape tannin
1 gallon boiling water
Yeast culture

Gather the flowers on a dry, sunny day and make sure they are fully open. Remove the green parts, and put the flowers in a 2-gallon plastic vessel with the peel only of the oranges and lemons. Add boiling water. Cover the vat and secure, stirring the mixture every 12 hours to keep flowers saturated. After 4 days, strain off the liquid and press the pulp. Add to the liquid all the other ingredients, including the juice of the oranges and lemons, stirring well to dissolve the sugar. Adjust the must to SG 1.100. Ferment to SG 1.030, and remove to a gallon jug with air lock. Rack in 3 weeks, then in 3 months. When the wine is clear, stabilize and bottle.

This recipe makes 5 bottles or 1 gallon —
all drinkable in a year.

Champagne, Cold Duck, and Canada Goose

The carbonic gas in bubbling wines disguises true flavors, so champagning is an excellent expedient for wines that are free of mildew and vinegar, but still do not taste quite up to snuff. For these sparkling wines, you will need 25 26-ounce pop bottles with crown cap tops and a capper.

1 5-gallon carboy of fully fermented wine
    that was started at SG 1.080 or less
    and has not been stabilized with
    sorbic acid
Water
Acid blend
10 ounces sugar
1 packet dry champagne yeast

If the wine you are using started at SG 1.090, add ⅛ of its volume in water, plus a level tablespoon of acid blend for each half gallon of water. If the wine you are using started at SG 1.095, add ⅙ its volume in water, plus acid blend at half a tablespoon per gallon of water.

Sterilize the bottles; then rinse them with plain water. In each bottle, place a rounded teaspoon of sugar and a few grains of the dry yeast. Fill the bottles to within 3 inches of the top. Cap with sterilized crown caps. Shake vigorously, and do so again on the seventh and thirtieth days. Before and after shaking, keep bottles upright.

After the thirtieth day, leave them for 2 months. At that point, remove a cap and check for fizz. If it's good, you can start drinking. If it's slightly torpid, you can start drinking anyway; but if you recap and wait another 90 days, your patience should be rewarded with more bubbles.

Cluett's Plonk is an excellent champagne base; the bubbly from it has been compared by cognoscenti to the champagne made at Chateau Margaux. Another interesting base for bubbly is a mixture of three or four different carboy ends brought together in a gallon jug when you are bottling; for this, you need only 5 bottles, 2 ounces of sugar, yeast, and 5 crown caps. The end product has been called Cold Duck and Canada Goose in North America and Hegel's Synthesis in Eastern Europe.

This recipe makes 24 bottles or 2 cases,
plus a test bottle.

Cider or Perry

A festive drink, 7½ percent alcohol, with a distinct pearl. Great for summer parties! To make this recipe you will need 5 26-ounce soda bottles and 5 crown caps.

3 pounds apples or pears
2 Campden Tablets
1 gallon boiling water
25 ounces sugar
3 teaspoons acid blend
1 teaspoon yeast nutrient
½ teaspoon grape tannin
½ teaspoon pectic enzyme
Yeast culture

Remove stems from fruit, cut the fruit into quarters, and crush it in a large plastic vessel. Dissolve Campden Tablets in the boiling water, and pour the water over the fruit, stirring the mix well. Tightly cover the vat. After 72 hours, pour off the liquid and press out the fruit. Add the sugar, acid blend, nutrient, and tannin. Adjust the must to SG 1.060. Then add the pectic enzyme and yeast culture. Cover. Stir twice daily for 5 days or so, measuring the SG daily. At 1.030, transfer the fermenting must to a glass vessel with air lock.

Continue to measure the SG at 2-day to 3-day intervals, until it reaches 1.010. At that point, transfer the wine to sterilized and rinsed bottles, capping them with sterilized crown caps. The bottles should be filled to within 3 inches of the cap. Store the bottles upright. When the liquid is clear, the cider or perry is ready to drink. When serving, be careful not to disturb the sediment on the bottom of the bottle.

This recipe makes 1 gallon or 5 bottles.

Elderberry Wine

6 ounces dried or 3½ pounds fresh
   elderberries
8 ounces raisins, chopped
2½ pounds sugar
4 teaspoons acid blend (optional)
1 teaspoon nutrient
2 Campden Tablets
1 gallon hot water
½ teaspoon pectic enzyme
Yeast culture
Vitamin C tablets

Combine the elderberries and raisins in a primary fermenter and add the sugar, acid blend, nutrient, Campden Tablets, and hot water. Cover. When the mix has cooled to 70° F., adjust the must to 1.100. Add the pectic enzyme and yeast culture. Cover with plastic sheet and secure with a string. Stir the must daily for 7 days. Strain out the fruit and siphon the liquid to a glass vessel with an air lock. *Do not press the fruit.* Pressed elderberries put out a hideous green gunk that ruins every piece of equipment with which it comes in contact. Beware.

Rack the wine in 3 weeks, again every 3 months. When the wine is clear and stable, bottle it, adding a 250 mg vitamin C tablet per gallon.

Makes 1 gallon or 5 bottles.

Potato or Carrot or Parsnip Wine

4½ pounds potatoes or carrots or
   parsnips
Peel and juice of 2 oranges
Peel and juice of 2 lemons
1 gallon boiling water
2½ pounds sugar
1 teaspoon yeast nutrient
½ teaspoon pectic enzyme
½ teaspoon grape tannin
Yeast culture

Scrub and dice the vegetables, removing the skins and all the discolored parts. Add the peel only of the fruit. Add the water and boil until the vegetables are tender. Let stand for 1 hour. Strain into a plastic vessel and add sugar. Cover. When the liquid is cool, add the other ingredients, including the juice of the oranges and lemons. (Some people at this point like to add ground ginger, ground cloves, and/or chopped raisins.) Adjust to SG 1.085. Stir daily for 5 days. Move to a glass vessel with an air lock. (If you added raisins, strain the wine first.) Rack in 3 weeks, again at 3 months. When the wine is clear, stabilize and bottle it. It will reach its peak of palatability in 6 to 15 months.

Makes 1 gallon or 5 bottles.

Raspberry or Plum Wine

This recipe will yield a dry and modest fruit wine of roughly 11 percent alcohol. Some rustics like both a more robust and a sweeter fruit wine. If you be one of these, increase the sugar to 3½ pounds, adding it 2 pounds at the beginning, 1 pound on the fourth day, ½ pound on the sixth day.

3 pounds fruit, de-stemmed and de-stoned
2 teaspoons acid blend
2 Campden Tablets
2 pounds sugar
1 gallon warm water (100° F.)
1 teaspoon yeast nutrient
½ teaspoon grape tannin
½ teaspoon pectic enzyme
Yeast culture

Crush the prepared fruit in a plastic vessel. Add all the ingredients, except the pectic enzyme and yeast. Stir thoroughly to dissolve the sugar. Cover with a plastic sheet. When the mix cools, adjust the must to SG 1.085. Add the pectic enzyme and the yeast culture. Cover and secure, stirring twice daily for 6 days. At that time, or whenever the must reaches SG 1.030, remove to a glass vessel and secure with an air lock. Rack in 3 weeks and again at 3-month intervals for 1 year; then stabilize and bottle the wine.

This recipe makes 1 gallon or 5 bottles.

Wheat Wine

Often a delight and a surprise. When made sweet — with 3½ pounds of sugar — it can be a very nice dessert wine.

1 pound whole wheat berries
1½ pounds raisins
1 gallon boiling water
Peel and juice of 1 lemon
Peel and juice of 2 oranges
2 pounds sugar
½ teaspoon acid blend
¼ teaspoon grape tannin
½ teaspoon yeast nutrient
¼ teaspoon pectic enzyme
Yeast culture

Crush the wheat, using a rolling pin and bread board, and add it with the chopped raisins to a 2-gallon vessel. Add boiling water, the peel only of the oranges and lemons, the sugar, the acid blend, tannin, and the nutrient. Move to a spot at room temperature.

When the mix cools, add the juice of the fruits. Adjust the SG to 1.100. Add the pectic enzyme, and the yeast culture. Cover and secure; stir daily for 5 days. After 7 days, strain (do not press) into a 1-gallon jug with air lock. Rack in 3 weeks and again in 3 months. Bottle the wine when it is clear and stable.

Makes 5 bottles or 1 gallon.

Ingredients for Winemaking

FRUIT	WEIGHT OF FRUIT TO YIELD 1 GALLON	PREPARATION OF FRUIT	WATER	ACID BLEND	CAMPDEN TABLETS
Apples	8 lb.	Crush	1 gal.	4 tsp.	2
Apricots	3 lb.	Destone	1 gal.	2 tsp.	2
Blackberries	4 lb.	Crush	1 gal.	1 tsp.	2
Blueberries	2 lb.	Crush	1 gal.	3 tsp.	2
Sweet cherries	4 lb.	Crush	1 gal.	3 tsp.	2
Sour cherries	3 lb.	Crush	1 gal.	2 tsp.	2
Cranberries	4 lb.	Crush	1 gal.	None	2
Concord grapes	6 lb.	Crush	1 gal.	None	2
California grapes	20 lb.	Crush	None	1 tsp.	2
Loganberries	2 lb.	Crush	1 gal.	2 tsp.	2
Peaches	3 lb.	Destone	1 gal.	3 tsp.	2
Plums	4 lb.	Destone	1 gal.	2 tsp.	2
Raspberries	3 lb.	Crush	1 gal.	2 tsp.	2
Strawberries	5 lb.	Crush	1 gal.	2 tsp.	2

Note: All teaspoon measures in this table are level teaspoons.

Ingredients for Winemaking (cont.)

YEAST NUTRIENT	SUGAR	RAISINS	PECTIN ENZYME	GRAPE TANNIN	WINE YEAST
1 tsp.	2 lb.	None	½ tsp.	¼ tsp.	1 pkt.
1 tsp.	2½ lb.	None	½ tsp.	¼ tsp.	1 pkt.
1 tsp.	2½ lb.	None	½ tsp.	None	1 pkt.
1 tsp. energizer	2½ lb.	1 lb.	½ tsp.	None	1 pkt.
1 tsp.	2½ lb.	None	½ tsp.	¼ tsp.	1 pkt.
1 tsp.	2½ lb.	None	½ tsp.	¼ tsp.	1 pkt.
1 tsp.	3 lb.	1½ lb.	½ tsp.	None	1 pkt.
1 tsp.	2½ lb.	None	½ tsp.	None	1 pkt.
None	None	None	None	None	1 pkt.
1 tsp.	3 lb.	None	½ tsp.	None	1 pkt.
1 tsp.	2½ lb.	None	½ tsp.	¼ tsp.	1 pkt.
1 tsp.	2½ lb.	None	½ tsp.	⅛ tsp.	1 pkt.
1 tsp.	2½ lb.	None	½ tsp.	¼ tsp.	1 pkt.
1 tsp.	2½ lb.	None	½ tsp.	¼ tsp.	1 pkt.

Adapted from *Making Homemade Wine*.

Universal Wine Recipe*

We offer you here the universal wine recipe chart of Mr. Stanley F. Anderson, of Vancouver, B.C. You will find it handy at times when you have picked a large quantity of ripe fruit that you want to ferment before it spoils — or when a quantity of ripe fruit has been dumped on you by a zealous acquaintance. The steps you should take are as follows.

1. Get a vessel (preferably plastic) that holds about 1½ times the volume of the crushed fruit. This can range from a 2-gallon plastic pail for 5 pounds of fruit to a 45-gallon plastic drum liner for 350 pounds of grapes.
2. Multiply or divide the quantities shown on the chart, and get the appropriate ingredients from a wine-makers' supply house, if you do not already have them. Get Andovin yeast if you can, otherwise use some other high-grade winemaker's yeast, and prestart it as explained on page 39.
3. Prepare the fruit as indicated on the chart.
4. Mix all the ingredients, crushing the Campden Tablets before adding them, and stirring the must well to dissolve the added sugar. Put it in a place that is between 65° and 75° F. Add the yeast culture.
5. Cover with a plastic sheet and secure with a string.
6. Stir twice a day and follow the outline in the section "Winemaking: Step by Step."

*This recipe first appeared in *The Art of Making Wine* by Stanley Anderson and Raymond Hull (Longman).

Used with permission.

Liqueurs as Gifts

Liqueur making is fun and easy and can be adjusted to your personal taste after minimal experimentation. Many people find commercial brand liqueurs too sweet; you may adjust the sugar content and find your lighter homemade versions just as tasty (sometimes better!) and a lot cheaper, too. Glycerine may be added for a thicker consistency. Note that the shelf life after maturation is 6 to 8 months, varying with each blend. Mark the date bottled and date to use by on the bottle to ensure maximum quality.

Liqueurs are not limited to use as an after-dinner drink. Many make a fantastic topping over ice cream, an exotic marinade or glaze, and a dessert treat when mixed in coffee. The possibilities in baking are numerous also.

Health food stores will have the best selection for many of the ingredients. Frozen, canned, or dried fruits may be used, but flavors will often not be as full. Herbs, nuts, and extracts may be added and/or substituted in recipes, creating an endless variety of combinations. Try a few basic recipes to develop a feel for proportions before experimenting.

Liqueurs should mature at least a week before drinking, preferably a month in most cases. Storing rounds out the taste, flavor, and brilliance, and gives an all-around better product. Keep a journal of ingredients, amounts, aging time, etc., for troubleshooting and to assure duplication. Batches may vary, however, for a variety of reasons. Fruit freshness can affect the taste as can shorter aging time. See Fine-tuning Your Liqueurs, page 58.

Equipment Needed

Empty widemouth jars, preferably dark glass and quart-size (i.e. juice, mayonnaise)

Cooking pot

Funnels

Blender or food processor

Strainer

Cheesecloth or similar material

Hammer or rolling pin (for crushing nuts)

Peeler or paring knife

Coffee or paper filters

Note: Widemouth jars are used because it is easier to remove the flavoring item (fruit, nuts, etc.). Use dark bottles when indicated in recipe. The indicated container sizes are only necessary when making the liqueur. It may be poured into smaller or more decorative bottles when done. It's a good idea to note on the bottle when started, shaken, stirred, etc. Also keep a record book of comments (less sweet, more fruit, just right, etc.) so individual taste preferences will be easier to achieve.

Steep, Strain, and Filter

The three steps repeatedly seen in the recipes are steep, strain, and filter.

Basically, steeping is the process used to give the alcohol its flavor. The alcohol absorbs the flavor of the other ingredients during the 1 to 4 weeks steeping period. Ideally, store the containers in a cool, dark place.

Once the alcohol has steeped, it needs to be strained to separate the liquid. Use a regular strainer and then restrain the fruit and nuts. Extract as much juice as possible; you will need either a fine wire mesh or cheesecloth-lined strainer to do so. An alternative method is to tie a piece of muslin or cheesecloth around the strainer and pour in the fruit. Lift off the cloth and twist to squeeze out the liquid. This can be a bit tricky, but is worth taking the time to do right because the fruit still holds much of the flavoring.

Finally, the liqueur needs to be fil-

tered. A clean finished product is what you are striving to achieve. Place a coffee or paper filter in a funnel and pour slowly, stirring filter to prevent clogging. Replace filter and repeat the process as necessary.

If you want to add different flavorings to your liqueur or strengthen the flavor if it is too weak, do so now and resteep another week. Continue then to add the sugar syrup, adjusting taste. Some liqueurs will need to age a few more weeks before serving, although others will be ready to enjoy immediately.

Fine-tuning Your Liqueurs

- Herb and spice flavorings are very potent so begin with a small amount — ¼ teaspoon to 2 teaspoons.

- Nuts and herbs must be crushed or broken to release full flavor.

- Be sure to scrape all white rind from orange and lemon peels or a bitter taste will result.

- Blot peels on paper towels to dry off oils and water.

- Ripeness of fruit can effect the final outcome of taste.

- If too weak, add more flavoring and resteep, or try ¼ teaspoon extract.

- To sweeten, the ratio is approximately 1 ounce to 4 ounces.

- If sour or bitter, add more sugar syrup.

- If too sweet, add a bit of lemon and resteep for a week.

- For a "créme de" liqueur, double the amount of sugar syrup.

- To thicken, add glycerine (1 to 2

teaspoons per quart); glycerine is available at most drugstores or winemaking shops.

Sugar Syrup

Sugar syrup is used for many of the following recipes. To make, the ratio is 1 part water to 2 parts sugar. Boil together for about 5 minutes at a full boil and be sure the sugar dissolves. The syrup MUST be cool before adding to the alcohol mixture as the heat evaporates the alcohol.

1 cup white granulated sugar
½ cup water

Yield: 1 cup.

Proportions

One cup sugar syrup plus 3 cups 80 proof vodka equals 60 proof liqueur. Two cups sugar syrup plus 3 cups 80 proof vodka equals 48 proof liqueur.

If a 100 proof vodka is used, increase the sugar syrup by ⅛ cup. For a "créme de" liqueur, double the amount of sugar syrup called for in the recipe. The greater the amount added, the lower the alcoholic content. Adjust sugar syrup to personal preference.

Fruit Liqueurs

Cherry Liqueur

Start looking for cherries from late April to August with June as the peak of the season. Pick plump, shiny, well-colored fruit with green stems, avoiding dark-colored stems. Do not rinse until use. Cherries are highly perishable so use as soon as ripe.

½ pound Bing cherries
½ pound granulated sugar
2 cups vodka

Wash, stem, and towel dry cherries and place in jar. Pour sugar over the cherries, following with the vodka. Unlike the other recipes, do not mix them. Place in widemouth quart jar. Cover with lid and store on shelf for 3 months without disturbing, then strain. Ready to serve. Recipe can be varied with extracts (chocolate, mint, orange, etc.). Add approximately 1 teaspoon of extract to finished liqueur and let sit another few weeks. Experiment with small portions of flavorings to find your desired taste.

Yield: 3 cups.

Orange Liqueur

Look for firm, heavy oranges which indicates lots of juice, and smooth-skinned ones free from soft spots or mold.

4 medium oranges*
1 vanilla bean
2 to 3 cups vodka
1 cup brandy
1 cup sugar syrup

Wash and peel oranges, making sure to scrape ALL white rind from the peels to avoid bitter flavor. Add to liquor and vanilla bean. Steep 2 to 3 weeks, strain and filter. Add sugar syrup and let age for 4 weeks in widemouth ½- or 1-gallon jar.

*The entire orange may also be used. Cut oranges into wedges and follow instructions. Gives opportunity to use tangerines, tangelos, or mandarin oranges. Cognac or brandy may be used as the base liquor and additional spices or extracts can be added.

Yield: 1 quart plus.

Peach Liqueur

Look for peaches from early May to mid-September with July and August as the peak months. You'll want yellow or cream-colored peaches. Avoid green ones as they won't ripen at home.

12 medium-sized peaches
4 strips lemon peel, scraped
1 stick cinnamon
3 cups vodka
1 cup sugar syrup

Peel peaches and cut in quarters. Combine with vodka, lemon peels, and spices in covered jar and store for 1 to 2 weeks in a widemouth gallon jar, shaking occasionally. Strain fruit (squeezing as much juice as possible) and filter. Add sugar syrup and store for an additional 6 weeks.

Yield: 1 liter.

Apricot Liqueur

2 cups smashed apricot pits
½ tsp. ground cinnamon
½ tsp. ground coriander
2 cups 100 proof vodka
1 cup sugar syrup

Partially fill a cloth bag (old pillowcase perhaps) with the apricot pits. They can be found at most health food stores. Pound with a hammer until they are smashed, using the crushed shell as well as the meaty center. Place smashed pits in a l-quart container.

Add cinnamon, coriander, and vodka. Store for 2 months in a cool, dark place. Filter through a cheesecloth-lined strainer and discard fruit pits. Strain a few times until clear. Sweeten with sugar syrup and age for two weeks in widemouth liter jar.

This recipe is for the inventive cook and requires some fine tuning, but it offers a feeling of accomplishment when done. Apricot extract can be added to offer additional flavoring.

Yield: 3 cups.

Raspberry Liqueur

Although July is the best month to buy raspberries, they can also be plentiful in May and June. Avoid stained baskets (sign of overripe or softened and decayed berries), and do not wash until ready to use as water causes mold to form. Berries should be full-colored and plump.

1 pint fresh raspberries
2½ cups vodka
1 vanilla bean
¼ teaspoon whole allspice
⅓ to ½ cup sugar syrup

Rinse berries and place in mixing bowl, lightly crushing to release flavor. Add vodka, vanilla bean, and allspice. Stir and store in widemouth quart jar in cool, dark place for 3 weeks. Strain mixture through dampened cheesecloth, squeezing as much juice as possible. Pour back in bottle, adding sugar syrup (to taste) and age another 3 to 5 weeks.

Yield: 1 pint plus.

Specialty Liqueurs

Almond Liqueur

3 ounces chopped almonds (unsalted)
⅛ teaspoon almond extract
1½ cups vodka
Dash of cinnamon
⅓ cup sugar syrup

Combine all ingredients and shake thoroughly. Let steep for 2 weeks in a quart jar. Filter and add more sugar if necessary. Let age for 2 more weeks and it will be ready to serve. Excellent in coffee or over ice cream.
Yield: 1 pint.

Vanilla Pecan

1 quart brandy
3 vanilla beans (2 inches)
One 6-ounce package pecans, chopped
2 cups sugar syrup
Pinch of cinnamon

Pour brandy, pecans, cinnamon, and vanilla beans (extract may be alternated) in a half-gallon jar and cover. Let stand for 2 to 3 weeks. Add sugar syrup to taste. Let stand 1 week. Strain and steep 2 more weeks. Ready to serve. Excellent for baking.
Yield: 1½ quarts.

Hazelnut Liqueur

6 ounces hazelnuts*
1 vanilla bean (1 inch)
Pinch of allspice
1½ cups vodka
⅓ cup sugar syrup

Chop the hazelnuts (releases the flavor of the nut) and add to vodka, vanilla bean, and allspice. Age for 2 weeks in a wide-mouth quart jar, shaking occasionally (lightly). Strain and filter until clear. Add sugar syrup, if desired, and age for 3 additional weeks. Ready to serve. Makes a nice gift during the holidays and is excellent over ice cream as well as an aperitif.

*Try using pistachios which also make a delicious liqueur. If flavor is too weak, add more nuts and resteep a week before adding the sugar syrup.
Yield: 1 pint.

Irish Cream Liqueur

3 eggs
1 tablespoon vanilla
2 teaspoons coconut extract
3 tablespoons chocolate syrup
One 14-ounce can sweetened condensed
    milk
2 cups Irish whiskey

Combine all ingredients in blender for 3 minutes. Refrigerate in a quart jar until thick, approximately 3 to 4 weeks. This recipe is not only easy to make, but is amazingly similar to the commercial brands. A favorite of most people!

Yield: 3 cups.

Coffee Liqueur

4 cups sugar
2 cups water
⅔ cup instant coffee
10 coffee beans (whole)
Fifth of vodka*
1 vanilla bean (2 to 3 inches)

Combine water, sugar, and coffee in a saucepan and bring to a full boil. Skim off the froth and allow to cool thoroughly. Pour into a half-gallon jar. Add vodka, coffee beans (optional, but will add a fuller flavor), and vanilla bean. Store in a dark place for 3 weeks. Strain and filter. Ready to serve.

*A brandy/vodka mix may be substituted for a simulated "Kahlua."

*A rum/vodka mix may be used to simulate "Tia Maria."

Yield: 1½ quarts.

Coconut Liqueur

2 cups packaged coconut
4 coriander seeds
¼ teaspoon vanilla extract
3 cups vodka
½ cup brandy

Add all ingredients together and steep in a widemouth quart jar for 3 to 4 weeks. Turn jar every few days. The coconut tends to be porous and absorbs the alcohol so be sure to thoroughly strain and filter the mixture to yield the largest amount. Natural coconut may also be used, but tends to be watery and requires more coconut.

Yield: 3 cups.

Herbal Liqueurs

Ginger Liqueur

½ cup crystallized ginger
2 cups vodka
½ cup sugar syrup

Add all ingredients together. Steep for 2 weeks in a quart jar. Strain and it is ready to serve. This liqueur has a real zing to it and will be enjoyed by a true ginger lover. Makes a unique addition to meat and poultry marinades.

Yield: 1 pint plus.

Peppermint Liqueur

2 to 3 teaspoons peppermint extract
3 cups vodka
1 cup sugar syrup

Combine all ingredients and stir. Let stand for 2 weeks in a quart jar. Use 2 teaspoons of extract for lighter mint taste and additional sugar syrup for a sweeter thicker liqueur.

Yield: 1 quart.

Licorice Liqueur

2½ tablespoons chopped licorice root
1½ cups vodka
½ cup sugar syrup to taste

Wash the licorice root and chop into small pieces. Add to vodka and steep for 1 week in a quart jar. Strain and filter. Add sugar syrup and steep for 1 week. Ready to serve. Adjust taste with extract if necessary.
Yield: 1 pint plus.

1. Chives   2. Sage
3. Fennel   4. Thyme
5. Tarragon 6. Mint

Making Flavored Vinegars

A totally different sort of bottled gift —
one guaranteed not to be duplicated.
Flavored vinegars are lovely, both to keep
for your own use and to give as special
gifts. There are many such vinegars on
the market, but yours will be better —
more flavorful, more unusual. (The price
difference is nice, too.) They are simple to
make. You're limited only by your own
imagination. Start by making the versions
given here, then create your own, adding
whatever herbs, spices, and flavorings
sound good to you.

After you have made one or two of
these unusual condiments, try them in the
recipes you'll find in other chapters of
Country Fresh Gifts (Blueberry Vinegar
Candy, page 100; Peach Vinegar Pie, page
96); or add one to three teaspoons to

soups, meat or poultry dishes, salads, or
seafoods. You'll find a number of such
recipes in *Making Flavored Vinegars* —
and you'll also be creating zippy new
versions of old family favorites that will
bring forth rave reviews.

Making these beautiful flavored
vinegars is fun, but using them is even
more fun. So then — you're *entitled* to
brag a little bit — make some for gifts.
Package them interestingly (see chapter
9) and present them with a copy of *Country
Fresh Gifts* or *Making Flavored Vinegars*.
And a smile!

Many flavored vinegars can be made
right in the bottles in which you will store
them or give them away — so long as you
have time to allow for the gradual buildup
of flavor by the steeping process. You
simply insert the flavoring ingredients into
the bottle, add the vinegar — and wait.

**What if you need to speed up the
process?** To do this, first bruise your
seasoning ingredients — smash them with
a garlic press, pepper mill or coffee
grinder, or even a hammer. (In the case of
fresh herbs, just crumple them up a bit.)
Then place them in a jar which has a cover
(an old mayonnaise jar, for example), heat
the vinegar you want to use to the boiling
point, and pour it into the jar.

Keep the jar at room temperature,
covered. Start tasting the vinegar in a day
or two (try a few drops on a small piece of
bread) so you will know when the flavor is
just right. In many cases, the vinegar will
be ready in just a few hours.

When you decide to go with the vinegar the way it is, strain out the flavoring
ingredients. Now examine the vinegar. If
it's cloudy, or has small particles, run it
through a coffee filter until it's clear.

Put another small supply of the seasoning ingredients (this time left whole) into the bottles, mostly for looks, and pour in the vinegar.

Other vinegars, such as raspberry, are best made by cooking the main ingredients briefly in the vinegar, then steeping. No matter which method you use, there's very little effort involved, and the rewards are tremendous.

All the vinegars will keep indefinitely. If you plan to keep them on hand for a long time, though, it's wise to sterilize the vinegar you use as a base to avoid further development of the cloudy-looking "mother." Because of vinegar's excellent preservative properties, any sprigs of herb, etc., you add will stay fresh looking.

The instructions below all make about 2 cups. To make more, just multiply all the ingredients as many times as you want.

What Base Vinegars to Use

In the instructions below, I suggest that you use a certain vinegar. There's always a reason for my choices. Red wine vinegar adds to the color of raspberry vinegar; white wine vinegar shows off the thyme, lemon peel and black pepper vinegar, and so forth. However, please feel free to follow your own inclinations.

Here are the vinegars you can find in most grocery stores. (You don't need to use the most expensive brands. You'll be making them special enough to please the most epicurean taste.)

Red wine vinegar — attractive to the eye; mildly gusty.

White wine vinegar — Off-white; delicate in taste.

Champagne vinegar — Not too different from white wine vinegar.

Japanese or Chinese rice vinegar (white or red) — Very subtle, delicate flavor (but be aware that the "seasoned" variety contains sugar).

Distilled white vinegar — Colorless; very acidic; best for such unsubtle uses as Hot, Hot, Hot Vinegar.

Apple cider vinegar — Light brown; strong flavor of apples.

Malt vinegar — Dark brown; very strong but pleasant flavor; can be hard to find except in Canada (where it's used on French fries!) or in England (where it's the preferred condiment for fish and chips).

Sherry vinegar — Brown; strong flavor of sherry; usually imported from Spain; rather expensive.

Of all these possibilities, the best for making most flavored vinegars are the first four — red wine, white wine, champagne and Japanese rice vinegars. For most purposes, the others have too strong a flavor of their own. (Exceptions: such pungent vinegars as the ones made with hot peppers, shallots, garlic, or onion.)

Recipes

Raspberry Vinegar

Many people consider this the very best of all the flavored vinegars. Because it's made with fresh fruit, the procedure is a little different from the usual. Don't omit the sugar or honey; this vinegar needs a touch of sweetening to bring out its full flavor.

2 to 2½ cups fresh red raspberries, lightly mashed (frozen raspberries can be used, but if they're pre-sweetened, don't add the sugar or honey)
2 tablespoons sugar or honey
2 cups red wine vinegar

Combine all the ingredients in the top of a non-aluminum double boiler. Place over boiling water, turn down the heat, and cook over barely simmering water, uncovered, for 10 minutes.

Place in a large screwtop jar and store for 3 weeks, then strain to separate the vinegar from the berries, pressing on the berries to get out all the juice. If your vinegar is cloudier than you wish, now run it through a coffee filter. Pour into the bottle(s) you plan to use, adding a few fresh berries.

Makes about 2 cups.

Shortcut: Paul Corcellet, maker of one of the finest commercial raspberry vinegars, also markets an excellent raspberry syrup which you can find in many fancy-food stores. A little of it added to some red wine vinegar will give you an instant raspberry vinegar which may not be quite as tasty as what you can make but is still very good.

Blueberry Vinegar

This ultra-chic and ultra-good fruit vinegar is made in exactly the same way as the raspberry vinegar above. Use either red or white wine vinegar.

Peach, Apricot, and Other Fruit Vinegars

Follow the same system for vinegars made from any fruit, but use white wine vinegar as the base. Can you imagine peach vinegar sprinkled on a fruit salad—or apricot vinegar mixed with mayonnaise and used in a chicken salad? I strongly recommend them.

Peel apricots, peaches, or nectarines before using by dipping them momentarily in boiling water, then removing the skin with your fingers. If they're big, cut the fruits immediately. Continue as you would for raspberry vinegar, above.

Herbal Vinegars

Your individual taste and the fresh herbs available to you will determine what you use in your herbal vinegars.

You can use one herb or a combination of as many as you like. In addition, you can combine herbs with other flavorings. I'll give you a few examples and numerous suggestions. After that, experiment!

I prefer white wine or white rice or champagne vinegar for all of these, simply because the herbs show up so well in them when you gaze admiringly at the bottles. Distilled white vinegar tends to overpower the herbs.

Basil and Other Single-Herb Vinegars

A pattern to follow — you can use any other fresh herb: dill, for instance, or chervil or — the greatest — tarragon. Chives make a subtle vinegar — use a lot of them. For small-leaved herbs such as thyme, use an extra sprig or two.

4 large sprigs fresh basil
2 cups white wine or champagne vinegar

Put the basil sprigs into a pint bottle and pour in the vinegar (or divide everything between two smaller bottles.) Seal. Store for 2 to 3 weeks before using.

Rosemary-Tarragon Vinegar and Other Herb-Combination Vinegars

If I had to pick a favorite of the herb vinegars, this would be it. Rosemary and tarragon are a terrific flavor combination, and the sprigs of the two herbs look fascinatingly exotic together.

Any herb goes well with any other herb. Oregano and dill are interesting together, as are basil and savory. You could use several herbs in combination.

2 large sprigs rosemary
2 large sprigs tarragon
2 cups white wine or champagne vinegar

Make this just as you would the basil vinegar above. If you're dividing it between two bottles, make sure to put a sprig of rosemary and a sprig of tarragon in each.

Hot, Hot, Hot Vinegar

Use with caution — though you can vary the fierceness of this vinegar by the number of hot peppers you use. Distilled white vinegar or apple cider vinegar are the ones to use here, because of their strength of flavor.

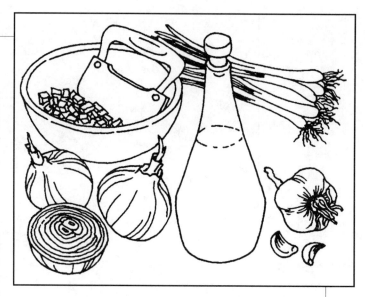

You will find this handy to have on hand. Not only will you have an instant source of hotness for certain Mexican and Oriental dishes, but you will also always be in possession of fresh hot peppers, since they keep perfectly in the vinegar. You can pull one out, cut off a little of it to use in cooking, then put the rest of it back into the bottle.

For the very hottest vinegar: Fill a jar with clean, dry, hot peppers. Pour in enough vinegar to cover. Seal. Store for a week or two before using. I use a mixture of jalapeños and the smaller, hotter serrano chilies, but you can use any hot fresh peppers you have or are able to find. *For a milder vinegar:* Use milder chilies (of course), and smaller amounts of them — or substitute pieces of red or green sweet peppers for part of the chilies. They will add flavor, but not heat.

Garlic, Shallot, or Onion Vinegar

Garlic, shallot, or onion vinegar is a good bet for giving a quick shot of pungency to almost anything nonsweet that you're cooking. Shallot vinegar is the mildest of the three and is usually well-liked by even those who run screaming at the thought of garlic. Onion vinegar isn't subtle at all, but that's fine. Garlic vinegar — well, garlic lovers think it enhances everything short of chocolate ice cream.

As to what vinegar to use: Garlic and onions seem to demand a vinegar with strength of its own: hence, good choices would be apple cider vinegar or white distilled. Shallots, being more delicate, get along well with wine vinegars.

⅓ cup chopped garlic, shallot or onion
2 cups vinegar (see above for the sorts to
    use)

Simply combine the chopped garlic, shallot, or onion with the vinegar in a screw-top jar. Store for 2 or 3 weeks, then strain and bottle, inserting the appropriate thing in each bottle — a peeled clove of garlic or shallot or either a piece of onion or a tiny white one, peeled.

Seven-Pepper Vinegar

Anything with a name this outrageous is fun to give as a gift, but this also happens to be a very good vinegar. Here's how you arrive at the large number of peppers:

Black peppercorns

White peppercorns

Szechuan peppercorns

Green peppercorns

Sweet green peppers

Sweet red peppers

Hot chili peppers (to make an Eight-
     Pepper Vinegar, you could add red
     and green hot peppers)

2 cups white wine vinegar

Make this vinegar exactly as you would Three-Pepper Vinegar, with these exceptions: Add the Szechuan peppercorns along with the black and white ones, then mince the sweet peppers and chilies very, very finely and add them to the vinegar at the same time as the green peppercorns. This does not need to be strained; the vinegar will preserve the fresh ingredients.

Szechuan peppercorns can be found in the Chinese foods sections of most supermarkets and, of course, in any Oriental market. They add much flavor but no heat.

Except as noted, material in this chapter has been excerpted and adapted from Making Homemade Wine *(A-75),* Making Flavored Vinegars *(A-112), and* Making Liqueurs for Gifts *(A-101), Storey/Garden Way Publishing Country Wisdom Bulletins.*

CHAPTER 4

Gifts of Bread

Making Sourdough

Baking with sourdough is being redis-
covered. In pioneer days, a pot of sourdough starter for leavening breads, bis-
cuits, and flapjacks was so commonly used
that no one would have thought of writing
a book of sourdough recipes. During the
California Gold Rush and the Yukon Gold
Rush, sourdough was so much a part of
their diet that the prospectors were called
"sourdoughs."

Sourdough is not uniquely American.
Columbus brought some to American
shores aboard his ship. The Egyptians
had it before the birth of Christ; the
ancient Greeks and Romans used it too.

If you have ever kept leftover mashed
potatoes or canned fruit so long it began to
ferment, you have an idea of how sourdough must have begun and of why it
attracted attention. The wild yeasts in the
air settle into such congenial environ-
ments as sugar, starch, and liquid combinations and begin to grow, fermenting and
producing potent alcohol which rises to

the top. For a long time people were more
interested in brewing than baking. Prospectors called this alcohol "hooch" after
the Alaskan Hoochinoo Indians who
produced liquor by a sourdough process.

Jokes about hooch and sourdough
permeate American humor. It is not
surprising that misconceptions about
sourdough developed and survive even
today. Perhaps the most common is that
starter should not be frozen. The fact is,
heat over 95° F. will kill the yeast; but
frozen, it keeps almost indefinitely and is
usable as soon as it has been thawed.
Freezing is probably the best way to
maintain a seldom-used starter.

Another belief is that sourdough is
finicky and that baking with it requires an
almost scientifically controlled environment. Obviously that can't be true or it
would not have flourished on wagon trains
and at prospecting sites where no one had
much control over temperature or time.

Another widely held, but mistaken,
idea is that anything baked with sourdough tastes so sour it puckers your

mouth. Actually, sourdough products can be as bland or as sour as you wish.

On the other hand, one thing about sourdough is true: Using it takes time. Sourdough needs more time to work as a leavener; so begin the baking process further ahead of when you want to finish than you would with commercial yeast or baking powder. That's the main way sourdough baking differs from other kinds. You must give sourdough time to grow, you have to keep it alive, and — of course — you have to have a starter.

Catching Sourdough Starter

There are four ways to catch the various kinds of wild yeasts suitable for food use:

1. Easiest is to scrounge a tablespoon or so of starter from someone else's flourishing pot.

2. Use commercial yeast, growing it in flour and warm water. Recipes follow.

3. Buy dried crystals of an existing sourdough strain and activate them following package instructions. (See p. 151, Suppliers.)

4. Start from scratch. Recipes and directions follow.

Once you have your starter, you keep it live by nourishing it with equal amounts of flour and warm water and letting it grow at room temperature. After it has worked for 4 to 24 hours, refrigerate it (or freeze some if you may not be using it for some time).

Starting from Scratch

4 cups unbleached white four
2 teaspoons salt
2 tablespoons honey
4 cups potato water

Mix all the ingredients together in a nonmetal container large enough to allow the mixture to double or triple in bulk. Let the mixture stand, covered, in a warm place (about 85° F. is ideal). In 2 or 3 days either the mixture will froth, expand, and smell sour, or it will mold and smell worse. If the first happens, you have captured wild yeast and created your own starter. Stir it down and refrigerate. Let it season a couple of days, then try baking with it to see if you like its flavor. (You may not. Some yeasts will leaven but they taste terrible.)

If you end up with a smelly, moldy bowl of flour and water, not a sign of bubble or froth to be seen, the catch has eluded you. Throw the mess away and try again, or try one of the other methods for getting a starter. The following recipe is more certain because it begins with dried or "domesticated" yeast.

Dried Yeast Starter

1 package active dried yeast
2 cups unbleached white flour
1½ cups warm water
1 tablespoon honey

Follow directions for Starting from Scratch. This will be better after aging; better yet after being used and replenished.

Whole Wheat Starter

1 package active dried yeast
1 cup whole wheat flour
1 cup warm water
1 tablespoon sugar

Follow directions for Starting from Scratch. Once the mixture has developed a slightly sour smell (about a day), refrigerate until you are ready to use it.

When you begin a starter in smaller amounts, as with this whole wheat starter, or when you find you are using your starter so often it hardly has time to ferment, you may need to expand your existing starter.

Expanding the Starter

To expand the amount of starter, simply add equal amounts of flour and warm water to it, let it ferment until it is bubbling and sour, then refrigerate. Some bakers keep two or more pots going so they can choose between a mild starter and an older, more pungent one, depending on what they are going to bake and how they want it to taste.

Sweetening the Pot

If your starter sits too long without new food for its yeast being added, it will become too sour and will lose its ability to leaven. To revive an overaged starter, you need to sweeten the pot.

Simply throw away all but a few spoonfuls of the old starter, wash the pot, and then mix the old starter with 2 cups each of flour and warm water. Let the mixture stand at room temperature until it bubbles and foams, as you did with the original

Using Sourdough in Baking

1. Use only clean, nonmetal utensils.

2. Use all ingredients at room temperature.

3. Allow time for the batter or dough (sponge) to rise before baking. Sourdough products don't expand in the oven as much as baking powder products do.

4. As you use the starter, replenish the volume used with equal amounts of flour and warm water. Let starter stand in a warm place (80° to 90° F.) until it ferments, bubbling and foaming. Then cover loosely and refrigerate. Let age one or two days if possible before the next use.

5. Freeze starter that isn't used often. Thaw it to room temperature when you're ready to use it again.

6. The tanginess characteristic of sourdough develops more the longer the sponge sits at room temperature. A mild flavor results from a few hours rising. A true, full, sourdough flavor develops after 24 hours or more.

starter. When the mixture is active, growing, and full of bubbles, return it to the refrigerator. For truest sourdough flavor let it age a day or so before you use it again. And next time, feed the starter a little sooner or, if you're not going to use it for a while, freeze it.

Replenishing the starter is merely a matter of putting into the pot about the same amounts of flour and water as you take out. The exact amounts don't matter; simply maintain about the same amount of starter all the time.

Adapting Recipes to Sourdough

To adapt a yeast recipe to sourdough, begin with a small amount of starter, about ¼ cup for recipes using less than 6 cups of flour and about ½ cup for recipes calling for more flour. Mix the starter with some of the flour and some of the liquid from the basic recipe you want to convert. Figure that ¼ cup starter has replaced about ¼ cup flour and slightly less than ¼ cup liquid in the recipe, and so on. In baking powder recipes figure the same way, but use as much as a cup of starter even in recipes calling for only 2 or 3 cups of flour.

Allow the mixture of starter, flour and liquid (the sponge) to stand and bubble for 4 to 24 hours, depending on the sourness you want. With quick breads you can shorten the time so the mixture stands only until it is obviously active, as little as an hour, if you're not trying for the sour taste. When ready to bake, proceed with the recipe, adjusting the amounts of flour and liquid according to the amount of starter you used. Add as much flour as necessary to get a dough you can knead or a batter (for quick breads) that seems about as thick as the recipe was before you adapted it to sourdough.

Go through the usual kneading, rising, and shaping steps for yeast breads. For quick breads, pour the batter into the pan and let it start to rise. Bake as usual.

Once you get used to it, you'll find it surprisingly easy to use sourdough in your own favorite recipes.

Note: Until you are accustomed to baking with sourdough, first review "Using Sourdough in Baking," on page 73, and "Adapting Recipes to Sourdough," page 74. Always allow for rising time.

Recipes are in chapters 4 and 5.

Bread Recipes

Bread has been with us since time immemorial, persisting through good reputation (. . . bread, a jug of wine, and thou . . .) and bad (but it's fattening!). And, so long as the sun shines upon the fields, bread, in its many guises, will be with us ever.

Sourdough White Sandwich Bread

This fine-grained bread has a tender crust and delicate texture because it's made with milk and allowed to rise twice before being shaped into loaves.

1 cup sourdough starter

1¼ cups unbleached white flour

1 cup warm water

1½ cups milk

2 tablespoons honey

2 teaspoons salt

2 tablespoons butter

6½ cups unbleached white flour, approximately

Mix the first 3 ingredients in a large bowl and allow to stand in a warm place so the mixture can ferment and bubble for 10 to 24 hours. When you are ready to bake the bread, heat the milk, add honey, salt and butter to it and cool the mixture to lukewarm.

When the liquid mixture reaches room temperature, mix in the sourdough mixture; then beat in enough flour to make a dough you can handle. Turn the dough out onto a floured board, cover with a damp cloth and allow to rest for 15 to 20 minutes before kneading. Knead until the dough is smooth and elastic. Don't skimp on kneading time.

After kneading, place the dough in a greased bowl and allow to rise until doubled in bulk. Cover the dough with a damp cloth to keep a crust from forming on it. Once the dough has doubled, punch it down, cover again with a damp cloth and allow to rise a second time to double. Each rising may take as long as 2 hours.

When the dough has doubled a second time, knead it down and shape into 2 or 3 loaves. Dough should fill each greased pan by about half. Brush loaves with melted butter, cover them with a damp cloth, and place in a warm spot to rise until double in bulk. This usually takes about an hour or so, depending on temperature.

Bake in a preheated 375° F. oven for about 45 minutes, or until the loaves are nicely browned, pull away from the sides of the pans, and sound hollow when tapped.

For the most tender crust, brush the loaves with butter again and cover lightly with a dry cloth as they cool.

Makes 2 or 3 loaves.

French-Style Sourdough Bread with Whole Wheat

Even people who ordinarily don't like whole wheat like this bread. It's especially good with stews, cheese fondue and baked beans.

½ cup starter

5 cups unbleached white flour

2 tablespoons oil

1 tablespoon honey

4½ cups warm water

5 cups whole wheat flour

1 tablespoon salt

3 to 5 cups unbleached white flour

Combine the first 5 ingredients in a large bowl. Cover loosely and allow to stand in a warm place 5 to 10 hours. The longer this sponge stands, the more sour the bread will be. When ready to make the bread, add the whole wheat flour and salt and mix well. Then gradually work in as much unbleached white flour as you need to make a dough you can handle.

Form the dough into a ball, cover with a damp cloth and allow to stand 15 to 20 minutes before kneading. Knead until smooth and elastic, place in a large, greased bowl in a warm place and allow to rise until double in bulk. If it is not convenient to bake the bread when it has doubled, punch down the dough and allow to rise again. When ready to bake, shape the dough into 5 long, skinny "ropes" and arrange them on a cookie sheet sprinkled heavily with corn meal. Put the loaves in a warm oven. When the bread starts to rise, turn the oven to 400° F. and bake until the crust is brown — about 25 minutes. For a traditional French look, slash the loaves 3 times each before baking; for heavier crust brush the loaves with cold water once or twice during the baking period and cool them, uncovered, on a rack.

Makes 5 small loaves.

Whole Wheat Bread

This is a basic hearty bread and the secret of its success is in kneading it until the dough is satiny.

3 cups warm water

2 cakes or tablespoons yeast

½ cup honey

6 to 7 cups whole wheat flour

¼ cup oil or melted butter

2 teaspoons salt

Place the warm water in a large mixing bowl and sprinkle in the yeast. Allow 5 minutes for the yeast to start bubbling. Stir in the honey, 3 cups of the flour, the oil, and the salt. Beat this mixture by hand until smooth. Slowly add the remaining flour cup by cup, until the dough becomes easy to handle. Turn the dough onto a lightly floured board and knead until it is smooth and satiny in texture. Use more flour if the dough is still sticky.

Place the dough in a lightly oiled bowl. Cover and let it rise in a warm place (85° F.) until it is double in bulk (about 1 hour). When doubled in bulk, punch it down, divide it into two parts and shape into loaves. Place into 2 greased loaf pans. Cover and let it rise again until it doubles in volume.

Bake in a preheated oven at 350° F. for 50 minutes or until the top is well browned. Remove from pans to cool.

Makes 2 loaves.

Adapted from *Cooking with Honey*.

Herb Batter Bread

Herbs in leaf or ground form tend to lose their flavor with prolonged cooking. Therefore, in herbal breads the flavor is likely to be quite mild unless seeds are used. Herbal seeds, and also spices, can be used to create flavorful breads. This bread is made from a batter, rather than a dough. Batter is stickier than dough and, therefore, requires very little kneading. I have always used instant minced onion in this recipe. I think the flavor is stronger than fresh onions and holds up better during baking.

1 tablespoon yeast

¼ cup warm water

1 cup low-fat cottage cheese

2 tablespoons sugar

2 tablespoons instant minced onion

2 tablespoons dill seed

1 tablespoon minced fresh dill weed

½ teaspoon dried oregano

¼ teaspoon baking soda

1 egg, unbeaten

1 tablespoon butter or margarine, softened

2¼ to 2½ cups all-purpose flour

Sprinkle the yeast over the warm water in a large bowl. While the yeast is dissolving, heat the cottage cheese to lukewarm in a medium-size saucepan. Stir constantly. Add all of the remaining ingredients, except the flour, to the warm cottage cheese. Stir until the ingredients are well blended. Add the cheese mixture to the yeast and stir well.

Add the flour ½ cup at a time, beating with a wooden spoon after each addition. Roll the dough onto a lightly floured counter and knead it 10 times until the dough is smooth and the flour absorbed.

Return the dough to the bowl and cover it with a damp towel. Place the bowl in a warm spot and let the dough rise until it has doubled in size (approximately 1 hour). Punch down the dough and shape it into a ball. Place it in a 1-quart, round casserole dish (8 inches) and let it rise for 30 to 40 minutes.

Preheat the oven to 350° F.

Bake for 40 to 50 minutes or until browned on top and hollow-sounding when tapped. Let the bread rest in the casserole dish for about 5 minutes. If you can wait, let the bread cool before slicing it. Hot bread tends to fall apart during slicing.

This flavorful bread goes well with mild cheeses and cold cuts. It is also a good accompaniment to hearty soups or stews on chilly nights.

Makes 1 round loaf.

Adapted from *Salt-Free Herb Cookery*.

Zesty Rye Bread

2 tablespoons yeast
1½ cups warm water
¼ cup molasses
1 tablespoon sugar
¼ cup orange juice
4 teaspoons fennel seed
4 teaspoons anise seed
½ teaspoon cardamom seeds
2 tablespoons grated orange zest
2 tablespoons unsalted butter or
    margarine, softened
2¼ cups rye flour
2 cups unbleached all-purpose white flour

Sprinkle the yeast over the warm water in a large bowl. In a small bowl mix the remaining ingredients, except the flours. When the yeast is dissolved, add the molasses mixture to the yeast and stir well.

Add the rye flour ½ cup at a time, beating with a wooden spoon after each addition. Then add the all-purpose flour in the same way. Roll the dough onto a lightly floured counter and knead for about 10 minutes, until the flour is absorbed and the dough is smooth, but not sticky.

Return the dough to the bowl and cover it with a damp towel. Let the dough rise in a warm place until it doubles in size (1 to 1½ hours). Punch down the dough and knead it several times to bring it back to its original size. Divide the dough in half and shape each half into a smooth oval. Place the loaves on a greased cookie sheet and let them rise for 1 hour.

Preheat the oven to 375° F.

Before baking, make three diagonal slashes across the top of each loaf. Bake for

30 minutes. Cool on racks.

This tasty bread blends beautifully with cheeses and sliced meats. It is delicious toasted and eaten with marmalade. A chilled soup, a crisp salad, and a slice of zesty rye bread make a memorable summer lunch.

Makes 2 oval loaves.

Adapted from *Salt-Free Herb Cookery*.

Sourdough Pumpernickel

¾ cup sourdough starter
1 cup unbleached white flour
¾ cup water
1½ cups milk
2 cups whole wheat flour
2 teaspoons salt
¾ cup corn meal
2½ cups rye flour, approximately

Mix together the first 3 ingredients in a large bowl, cover loosely and allow to ferment in a warm place for at least 10 hours, longer if you want a sour pumpernickel. When you are ready to bake, mix the milk (which should be lukewarm) into the fermented starter mixture, then beat in the whole wheat flour, salt, and corn meal. Next, work in as much rye flour as needed to make a dough you can handle. Shape it into a ball, cover with a damp cloth and allow to stand for about 20 minutes before you try to knead it. This bread is difficult to knead and you may find it easier if you grease your hands well before beginning.

When the dough is thoroughly kneaded,

place it in a greased bowl, turning it once so the top of the ball of dough is also greased. Set the dough in a warm place, covered with a damp cloth, to rise.

This bread will rise slowly because it is heavy, so allow an hour or more. When the dough feels light and puffy, even if it has not quite doubled in bulk, knead it down and form into a round loaf. Put the loaf on a cookie sheet which has been heavily sprinkled with corn meal, grease the top of the loaf with soft butter, and place in a warm spot to rise until nearly double. This will probably take at least an hour.

Bake in a preheated 375° F. oven for about 40 minutes, or until the loaf sounds hollow when you tap it.

This makes a very dense loaf; if you would prefer it a little more springy, substitute unbleached white flour for some of the whole wheat flour and be sure to allow plenty of rising time before baking.

Makes 1 round loaf.

Raisin Bread

Whole Wheat Bread Recipe — substitute half or all of the whole wheat flour with unbleached white flour
6 tablespoons melted butter
½ cup warmed honey
1 cup raisins
4 teaspoons cinnamon
2 tablespoons melted butter

Prepare the dough as for the bread recipe. After the dough has risen once, punch down and divide it in two. Roll each piece of dough on a floured board into an oblong shape, ¼ inch thick. Spread each piece with the melted butter, honey, raisins, and cinnamon. Separately roll each piece of dough up as for a jelly roll and pinch the seams to seal. Tuck the ends under and put each loaf in a well-greased bread tin. Brush the top of each loaf with a tablespoon of melted butter. Bake in a 350° F. oven for 45 to 50 minutes until golden brown. Remove from the pans to cool.

Makes 2 loaves.

Adapted from *Cooking with Honey*.

Sourdough Zucchini Bread

Here's a quick bread recipe for midsummer when zucchini takes over the land, causing frugal cooks and gardeners to whip up everything from zucchini tarts to zucchini ice cream sundaes to keep from wasting any of the prolific squash. This zucchini bread is similar to the standard quick zucchini breads you may have tasted, except the sourdough gives it a definitive tang and makes it a more moist loaf.

½ cup oil

¾ cup brown sugar

1 egg

½ cup sourdough starter

½ cup milk

1 cup grated zucchini squash

2 cups unbleached white flour

½ teaspoon each baking powder and
    baking soda

½ teaspoon salt

1 teaspoon cinnamon

¼ teaspoon ground cloves (optional)

¼ cup raisins

¼ cup chopped nuts

Preheat oven to 325° F. Mix the oil, sugar, egg, starter, and milk together in a large bowl. Stir until the sugar is fairly well dissolved. Add the grated zucchini and mix well. Sift the dry ingredients together into the zucchini mixture. Gently fold in the raisins and nuts.

Turn this batter into a greased and floured loaf pan large enough that the mixture does not fill it by more than two-thirds. Bake for about an hour, or until the loaf tests done when you poke it with a toothpick. Cool at least 5 minutes before removing the loaf from the pan, then cool completely on a rack. For best flavor and texture, wrap the loaf after it is completely cooled and do not cut it until the next day.

Makes 1 loaf.

Banana Bread

⅔ cup honey

½ cup oil

3 eggs, beaten

3 ripe bananas, mashed

¼ teaspoon salt

1 teaspoon vanilla

2 cups unbleached flour or whole wheat
    pastry flour

1 teaspoon baking soda

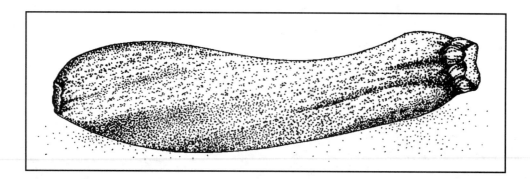

Preheat oven to 350° F. Beat together the honey and oil, then add the eggs. Add the mashed bananas, salt, and vanilla; mix well.

Sift together the flour and baking soda. Gradually blend the flour mixture in with the banana mixture until the batter is smooth. Grease 1 large or 2 small loaf pans, pour in the batter, and bake for 45 to 60 minutes depending on the size of the pan. Lower the oven temperature if the bread is browning too quickly.

Makes 1 large loaf, or 2 small ones.

Adapted from *Cooking with Honey*.

Apple Crescent Loaf

This is my favorite yeast bread. I use it around the holidays when friends drop in.

Yeast Dough:

1 cake or tablespoon yeast

1 cup milk scalded, cooled to lukewarm

¼ cup honey

3 tablespoons oil or melted butter

½ teaspoon salt

2 eggs, beaten

2 cups unbleached white flour

1½ cups whole wheat flour (do not use whole wheat pastry flour)

3 tablespoons melted butter

Apple Filling:

4 apples

2 tablespoons water

½ cup raisins

½ cup walnuts (optional)

¼ cup honey, warmed slightly

1½ teaspoons cinnamon

Soften the yeast in milk with 1 teaspoon of the honey in a small bowl. Blend the rest of the honey, butter or oil, salt, and eggs in a large bowl. Add the yeast and milk and stir in the white and whole wheat flours. Turn the dough onto a lightly floured board and knead lightly, adding a small amount of flour if necessary. Turn into a lightly oiled bowl, cover, and let rise until double in bulk — about 1 hour.

Peel, slice, and stew the apples in 2 tablespoons of water until soft. Allow to cool slightly.

Roll out the dough into an oblong shape, ¼ inch thick. Brush with 2 tablespoons of melted butter. Spread the apples, raisins, and nuts over the dough. Drizzle the honey over the apples and sprinkle on the cinnamon. Roll the dough up as for a jelly roll. Put it on a greased cookie sheet and shape into a crescent, turn the ends under and slit the top in a few places to expose the filling. Cover and set in a warm place to rise slightly.

Brush the top with the remaining tablespoon of butter and bake in a 375° F. oven for about 30 minutes.

Makes 1 loaf.

Adapted from *Cooking with Honey*.

Lemon Basil Tea Bread

⅓ cup melted butter

1 cup sugar

2 eggs

¼ teaspoon almond extract

1½ cups white flour

1 teaspoon baking powder

½ cup milk

2 tablespoons lemon basil leaves

1 tablespoon grated lemon peel

3 tablespoons fresh lemon juice

2 tablespoons sugar

Preheat oven to 325° F.

In a bowl, blend together the butter and the cup of sugar. Beat in the eggs, one at a time. Stir in the almond extract. Sift the flour and baking powder into the egg mixture, alternately adding the milk. Fold in the lemon basil leaves and lemon peel. Stir to blend. Turn the batter into a greased 8½ x 4½-inch ovenproof loaf pan. Bake for about 60 minutes, or until the loaf tests done in the center. Remove the loaf from the oven, and place on a rack to cool.

Meanwhile, mix together the lemon juice and the 2 tablespoons of sugar in a small bowl. Prick the top of the lemon bread with a fork in several places, then pour the lemon and sugar mixture over the loaf.

Makes 1 loaf.

Adapted from *Growing and Using Basil*.

Fruit Scones

Every time I bite into scone bread, I step right back into my English childhood. My mother used to bake this each morning so that there would be a nice fresh piece for our school lunch boxes.

1½ cups unbleached flour

¾ teaspoon baking soda

½ teaspoon baking powder

¾ cup whole wheat flour

¼ cup sugar

6 tablespoons butter or margarine

1 large egg

¾ cup plain yogurt

½ cup raisins or chopped dates

Preheat the oven to 425° F.

Sift the unbleached flour, baking soda, and baking powder into a large bowl. Add the whole wheat flour and sugar. Mix together. Cut the butter into several pieces and rub into the flours with your fingertips until the texture resembles peas.

In a small bowl, beat the egg, stir in the yogurt and raisins. Pour into the flour mixture and, using a fork, stir until a soft dough is formed.

Lightly flour a baking tray. Scoop the dough onto the tray and pat into a round approximately ¾ inch thick. Bake for 20 minutes or until a skewer, inserted in the center, comes out clean.

Serve warm with butter and jam. This also makes a delicious dinner bread — substitute 1 tablespoon of dried herbs for the raisins.

Yield: 6 to 8 servings.

Adapted from *Cooking with Yogurt*.

Crackers, Bagels, and Pretzels

Sourdough Sesame Crackers

½ cup sourdough starter
2 tablespoons butter
2 teaspoons salt
1 cup unbleached white flour
¼ cup sesame seeds (preferably unhulled)

Allow the starter to stand at room temperature for several hours until it is frothy and active. Melt and cool the shortening and add it to the starter, along with the salt and as much of the flour as you can work in. When you have a very stiff dough, turn it onto a floured board and knead in the sesame seeds and, if needed, flour. This will be easier to do if a few minutes before kneading you allow the dough to rest, covered with a damp cloth.

When you have a very stiff dough roll it to a uniform thickness of about ⅟₁₆ inch. Don't worry if the dough doesn't hold all the sesame seeds. Cut the crackers with a sharp, round cutter and arrange them on an ungreased cookie sheet, leaving space between each cracker. Stick them full of holes with a fork and bake in a preheated 400° F. oven for about 7 minutes. The crackers should brown lightly, but don't let them over-brown.

Cool the crackers on wire racks. If you can get them put away before everyone gobbles them, store them in an airtight tin.

Bagels

2 cups whole wheat flour
2 to 3 cups unbleached white flour
1 tablespoon salt
3 tablespoons honey
1 tablespoon yeast
1½ cups very warm water
1 egg white, beaten
1 tablespoon cold water

In a large bowl, thoroughly mix 1 cup whole wheat flour, ½ cup unbleached flour, salt, honey, and undissolved yeast. Gradually add warm tap water and beat for 2 minutes with an electric beater at medium speed. Add ½ cup unbleached flour. Beat at high speed for 2 minutes. By hand, stir in enough additional flour to make a soft dough. Turn onto a lightly floured board; knead until smooth and elastic.

Place the dough in an ungreased bowl. Cover and let rise in a warm place for about 20 minutes. (The dough will not double in bulk.) Punch down. Turn onto a lightly floured board.

Cut the dough into 12 equal parts. Roll each piece into a long strip. Pinch the ends of the strip together to form a circle. Place on an ungreased baking sheet. Cover and let rise for 20 minutes.

Boil 2 inches of water in a shallow pan. Lower the heat and add a few bagels at a time. Simmer for 7 minutes. Remove from the water and place the bagels on a towel to cool. Cool for 5 minutes. Preheat oven to 375° F.

Place the bagels on ungreased baking sheets. Bake for 10 minutes. Remove from the oven and brush the tops with the combined egg white and cold water. Return to the oven and bake about 20 minutes, until golden brown.

Makes 12 bagels.

Adapted from *Cooking with Honey.*

Sourdough Pretzels

These pretzels are absolutely delicious. They're the kind you sometimes can buy from street vendors in cities, and they're wonderful with a little mild yellow mustard squirted on just before you eat them.

¾ cup sourdough starter

¾ cup unbleached white flour

½ cup water

2 tablespoons butter

3 tablespoons sugar

2 teaspoons salt

1 cup hot water

5½ cups unbleached white flour,
    approximately

1 egg yolk

2 tablespoons heavy cream

Coarse salt

Combine the first 3 ingredients in a large bowl, cover loosely and allow to stand in a warm place at least 8 hours. When ready to make the pretzels, dissolve the butter, sugar, and salt in the hot water and cool to lukewarm. Add it to the starter mixture and gradually beat in 4 cups of flour. When the dough is stiff and well-mixed, turn it out onto a floured board and let it rest a few minutes. Knead in more flour until you have a very stiff dough. Put the dough in a greased bowl, turn once to grease the dough and cover with a damp cloth. Let the dough rise in a warm place for 2 hours.

Shape pieces of dough into long ropes, then twist the ropes into pretzel shapes on a greased cookie sheet. Brush the pretzels with a mixture of the beaten egg yolk and cream. Cover with a damp cloth and allow to rise in a warm place for about half an hour. Preheat oven to 425° F. Brush pretzels with the egg mixture again, sprinkle with salt and bake about 15 minutes.

Cool the pretzels before serving because they'll be gummy when they're hot.

Except as noted, material in this chapter has been excerpted and adapted from Baking with Sourdough, *Storey/Garden Way Publishing Country Wisdom Bulletin A-50.*

CHAPTER 5

Just Desserts

Using Honey in Foods

After we began to raise bees, I gradually switched from cooking and baking with sugar to preparing food entirely with honey. I found that I could use honey to replace all or some of the sugar in almost any recipe, if I followed a few simple rules.

Honey is available in several forms:

- Comb honey. Honey can be left in the wax combs, just as the bees store it. Comb honey is delightful to eat, wax and all, spread on a warm slice of fresh bread or a muffin. Since the bees have sealed it in wax, it keeps all the original flavor months later.

- Liquid honey. This honey is spun from the combs and bottled. Most commercial honey is warmed before bottling so it will remain liquid. Liquid honey is the easiest and most commonly used form for cooking.

- Crystallized honey. This is extracted honey which has been bottled unheated. It will undergo a natural process of granulation and will retain its original flavors better than heated

honey. It has a nice, easily spread consistency, and many people prefer their honey this way when they become familiar with it. Warm it slowly in its container in a pan of water to reliquefy crystallized honey.

There are as many flavors of honey as there are flowers. Generally, the lighter the honey, the milder is its flavor and the better it is for general cooking.

Cooking Tips:

- Honey is a liquid sweet that adds its own special flavor to foods. It tends to absorb moisture, which enables baked goods to stay fresher longer.

- Substitute the honey cup for cup of sugar, but decrease the amount of liquid in the recipe by ¼ cup.

- If you find that honey is too sweet cup for cup of sugar, substitute ¾ cup of honey for each cup of sugar and reduce the amount of liquid by 2 to 3 tablespoons.

- Measure the honey in a cup after the oil or fat in a recipe, or coat the cup or spoon with oil. This keeps the honey from sticking, so you get it all out.

- Honey is acidic. In baked goods where as much as 1 cup of honey is being substituted for sugar, if no baking soda is called for, add ½ teaspoon of baking soda.

- Honey works best in most recipes as a liquid. It can then be added slowly to the other liquid ingredients in the recipe.

- Crystallized honey can be measured cup for cup of liquid honey; the two can be used interchangeably in cooking. But crystallized honey tends to make baked goods denser. What I do is measure the crystallized honey in a metal measuring cup, put the metal cup in a pan of warm water, double-boiler style, until the honey liquefies. Then I add the liquid honey to my ingredients after it is cooled.

- When substituting honey for sugar in a recipe, bake the food longer and at an oven temperature 25° F. lower than the original recipe called for.

- Most honey breads and cakes improve in flavor and texture if they are baked and wrapped a day before eating.

- Never add another substance to honey that you intend to store. Unadulterated and covered, it will keep at room temperature for — literally — centuries.

Adapted from *Cooking with Honey*.

Cake Recipes

Sourdough Chocolate Cake

Few people bother to bake cakes from scratch anymore unless they can produce something that's not possible with a mix. This sourdough chocolate cake falls in that category. It's got a fudgelike quality you can't get any way except with sourdough and since it's all mixed in one bowl, it's almost as easy as a boxed cake.

½ cup sourdough starter
1½ cups all purpose white flour
2 cups sugar
¾ cup powdered cocoa (not instant)
1 teaspoon baking powder
2 teaspoons baking soda
2 eggs
1 cup milk
½ cup vegetable oil
¾ cup cold coffee
1 teaspoon vanilla

Put the starter in a large bowl, cover loosely and allow to stand at room temperature until active and bubbling — at least an hour. Then add the rest of the ingredients, in the order given, beating well after each addition. It is not necessary to sift or premix any of the ingredients as long as you are careful to get the baking powder and baking soda evenly mixed.

Grease and flour two 9-inch round cake pans, pour in the batter, which will be thin, and bake in a preheated 350° F. oven for about 30 minutes, or until the layers test done when poked with a toothpick. The cake will have pulled away from the sides of the pan.

Allow to cool about 10 minutes before removing from pans, then finish cooling the layers on wire racks. Do not frost until the cake is completely cold.

A mild chocolate butter cream frosting is nice with this cake.

Simmer chopped green tomatoes and ½ cup sugar until tomatoes are well cooked and transparent. Strain through a colander or sieve to remove seeds, cores and skins. There should be 1¼ cups pulp. Cool. Preheat oven to 350° F. Cream remaining 1 cup sugar and shortening until fluffy. Add the eggs. Blend soda into cooled tomato pulp and add gradually to creamed mixture, beating well after each addition. In a separate bowl, combine salt, spices and flour. Gradually add all but one cup of the flour mixture to the batter, beating well. Finally, add raisins and nuts to remaining 1 cup flour and mix to coat well. Add, all at once, to batter and beat well. Pour into a well-greased and floured square cake pan and bake 35 to 40 minutes, until lightly browned and the touch of a finger does not leave an impression. Serve plain or frosted.

Adapted from 52 Great Green Tomato Recipes.

Green Tomato Spice Cake

2 cups green tomatoes, chopped

1½ cups sugar

½ cup vegetable shortening

2 eggs, beaten

2 teaspoons baking soda

1 teaspoon salt

1 teaspoon powdered cinnamon

½ teaspoon ground nutmeg

½ teaspoon powdered cloves

2 cups flour

½ cup seedless raisins

½ cup walnuts, chopped

Carrot Cake

¼ cup butter, softened
½ cup oil, mild in flavor
¾ cup honey
2 eggs, beaten
1¼ cups unbleached flour
1 teaspoon baking soda
1 teaspoon cinnamon
1½ cups grated carrots
½ cup coconut
½ cup walnuts

Preheat oven to 350° F. With an electric mixer, blend the butter and oil. Slowly pour in the honey and eggs (one at a time) while mixing. Combine the flour and baking soda and sift into the liquid. Add the cinnamon. Stir in the grated carrots, then the coconut, and finally the chopped nuts. Pour the batter into a well-greased 8 x 8-inch pan and bake for 35 minutes.

Serves 9.

Adapted from *Cooking with Honey*.

Honey Cream Cheese Icing

2 tablespoons honey
8 ounces softened cream cheese

Beat the honey into the softened cream cheese until smooth and well blended. Spread on a cooled cake. Refrigerate the cake if this icing is used.

Makes enough frosting for one 8 x 8-inch cake.

Adapted from *Cooking with Honey*.

Simple Sour Cream Cake

¼ cup butter or margarine, room
    temperature
1½ cups brown sugar, packed
2 eggs
1 teaspoon vanilla extract
2 cups flour
½ cup wheat germ (or omit and increase
    flour ⅓ cup)
1 teaspoon baking soda
1 teaspoon salt
4 cups rhubarb, cut into ½-inch pieces
1 cup sour cream

Topping:

½ cup sugar
1 teaspoon cinnamon
1 cup nuts, chopped

Preheat oven to 350° F. Cream butter and sugar. Beat in eggs and vanilla. Sift flour, wheat germ, baking soda, and salt together. Combine with batter mixture. Add rhubarb and sour cream. Pour thick, well-blended batter into a greased 9 x 13-inch baking pan.

For topping combine sugar, cinnamon, and nuts. Sprinkle on batter. Bake 40 minutes, or until cake passes toothpick test. Serve with whipped cream, if desired.

Serves 10.

Adapted from *Great Rhubarb Recipes*.

Mennonite Upside-Down Cake

2 tablespoons butter or margarine
1 cup brown sugar
2 cups fresh rhubarb, diced
¼ cup cooking oil
1 cup sugar
1 egg
2 cups flour
2½ teaspoons baking powder
½ teaspoon salt
1 cup milk
Cream or whipped cream

Preheat oven to 375° F. Melt butter or margarine in baking pan. Add brown sugar and rhubarb. For batter, combine oil and sugar. Add egg and beat. Sift flour; measure, then sift flour with baking powder and salt. Add dry ingredients alternately with milk. Pour over rhubarb. Bake cake for 40 to 45 minutes. May be served with cream or whipped cream.

Serves 6.

Adapted from *Great Rhubarb Recipes*.

Sourdough Cherry Cobbler

If you prefer, make your own filling according to any standard cherry pie filling recipe.

1 can cherry pie filling (1 lb. 5 oz.)
½ cup white raisins
¼ cup sourdough starter
¾ cup white flour
½ cup brown sugar
½ cup granulated sugar
¼ cup butter
½ cup chopped pecans

Preheat oven to 425° F. Grease an 8-inch round pie plate or cake pan. Put in the cherry filling and scatter raisins evenly over top of the cherries. Bring the sourdough starter to room temperature. When it is active and bubbling you can begin to mix the cobbler topping. Sift together the dry ingredients and cut in the butter until the mixture resembles coarse meal. Stir in the starter and the pecans. Mix thoroughly but lightly. Spoon the starter mixture over the top of the cherry filling, working in circles from the outer edges of the pan and leaving a small uncovered circle in the center.

Bake for 25 minutes, or until the top is lightly browned and the cherry filling is bubbling up through the center. Serve barely warm with vanilla ice cream on top.

Makes 6 to 8 servings.

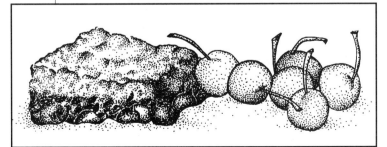

Silver Scented Geranium Cake

One of the adventures in cooking is to branch out in a totally new direction. Try this delicate-tasting white cake that uses the leaves of scented geraniums for flavor and fragrance. Your favorite butter cream frosting would be good — but serve it first grandly on its own. This is from a famous dining establishment, The Heritage Restaurant in Cincinnati.

¼ cup soft butter

¼ cup shortening

1⅓ cups sugar

2 teaspoons vanilla

2¼ cups cake flour

3 unbeaten egg whites

2½ teaspoons baking powder

¾ teaspoon salt

1 cup milk

Line 9 x 12-inch pan with wax paper, then cover wax paper with leaves of scented geranium (Attar of Rose for rose scent or Mabel Grey for lemon scent). Set oven at 375° F. Cream butter and shortening with wooden spoon until smooth. Add sugar; stir in flavoring. Add egg whites and beat vigorously until fluffy. Add flour (sifted together with baking powder) alternately with milk, ending with flour mixture and rest of milk. Pour into pan carefully. Bake 20 minutes or until done.

By courtesy of Janet Melvin. Adapted from *Growing & Using Scented Geraniums.*

Substituting Yogurt for Cream Cheese in Cheesecake

If a cheesecake recipe calls for three 8-ounce packages of cream cheese, drain 9 to 10 cups of yogurt for 6 to 8 hours to get 3 packed cups. Since most cheese-cake recipes include flour and/or eggs, there will be no need to stabilize the yogurt — it will act just like cream cheese — for fewer calories.

Adapted from **Cooking with Yogurt.**

Cookies and Bars

Gingerbread Men

½ cup softened butter

6 tablespoons honey

¼ cup blackstrap molasses

2 cups unbleached flour

1½ teaspoons baking soda

1½ teaspoons cinnamon

1½ teaspoons ginger

Preheat oven to 375° F. Combine the butter, honey, and molasses. Add the dry ingredients and stir until a dough is formed. Divide the dough in half and knead each ball gently. This dough is soft and buttery. Roll each ball to a thickness of ¼ inch on a lightly floured board and cut out the dough with a cookie cutter. Place on a greased cookie sheet. Bake for 5 to 7 minutes. Watch carefully since they burn easily. Decorate with your favorite icing.

Makes 12 men.

Adapted from *Cooking with Honey.*

Old-Fashioned Filled Cookies

Cookie Batter:

1½ cups sugar

½ cup butter or margarine

1 egg, well beaten

½ cup milk

3½ cups flour

2 teaspoons baking soda

2 teaspoons cream of tartar

½ teaspoon salt

Cream sugar and butter or margarine until fluffy. Add egg and milk and blend well. In a small bowl combine flour, soda, cream of tartar, and salt. Add to creamed mixture and blend well. Chill at least 1 hour.

Filling:

½ cup sugar

1 tablespoon cornstarch

1½ cups canned or fresh green tomatoes, chopped and drained

Grated rind and juice of 1 lemon

In a saucepan, combine sugar, cornstarch and tomato pieces. Cook over low heat, stirring constantly, until very thick. Add grated rind and juice of lemon, stir well and heat again to bubbling. Chill.

Preheat oven to 350° F.

To assemble cookies, roll chilled dough to ⅛-inch thickness and cut cookies with the outer ring of a doughnut cutter or cookie cutter. Top half the cookies with 1 tablespoon chilled filling. Using the center ring of doughnut cutter or a thimble, cut the center from the remaining half of the cut-out cookies and place on top of filled halves. Crimp edges with a fork to seal and bake 15 to 20 minutes, until lightly browned.

Makes 3 to 4 dozen cookies.

Adapted from *52 Great Green Tomato Recipes.*

Honey Date Bars

Filling:

½ pound pitted dates, cut in pieces

½ cup honey

¼ cup water

Dough:

1 cup rolled oats

1 cup unbleached flour

¼ teaspoon salt

½ cup honey

½ cup butter, melted

½ teaspoon cinnamon

Put the dates, honey, and water in a pan and cook slowly until thickened. Allow to cool. Preheat oven to 325° F.

Combine the oats, flour, salt, honey, butter, and cinnamon in a bowl. Mix well.

Pat half of the oat mixture on the bottom of a greased 8-inch by 8-inch pan. Spoon all of the filling on the oat mixture. Top with the other half of the dough. Spread the dough with a knife to cover all of the date mixture. Bake for 30 minutes. Cut into squares while warm.

Makes 16 squares.

Adapted from *Cooking with Honey.*

Rhubarb Bars

2 cups flour

1 cup margarine, melted

½ cup plus 2 tablespoons confectioners' sugar

4 eggs, beaten

2 cups sugar

½ cup flour

¾ teaspoon salt

4 cups rhubarb, diced

Preheat oven to 350° F. Combine flour, margarine, and confectioners' sugar. Pour into 9 x 13-inch baking pan. Bake 15 minutes. Combine eggs, sugar, flour, and salt. Fold in diced rhubarb. Pour mixture over crust. Bake 45 minutes.

Makes 18 bars.

Adapted from *Great Rhubarb Recipes.*

Pies

Yogurt Berry Pie

1 cup unbleached flour
8 tablespoons butter or margarine (1 stick)
2 to 3 tablespoons cold water

Filling:

2 cups of berries (strawberries,
    raspberries, or blueberries)
½ cup sugar or ⅓ cup honey
2½ tablespoons cornstarch
2 cups plain yogurt, drained 30 minutes
    or more to yield 1 cup

To make the pie shell, pour the flour into a large bowl or food processor. Cut the butter into thin slices, and drop into the bowl. Using a pastry blender, two knives, or the processor, work the mixture until it has the texture of large crumbs. Pour in the cold water, and mix until the pastry forms a ball. Remove from the bowl, place on a piece of wax paper, and flatten the dough into a 6-inch circle. Cover and refrigerate for 15 to 30 minutes.

Meanwhile, make the filling by placing the berries in a saucepan over low heat. Mix the sugar and cornstarch together, and stir into the berries. Cook over medium heat, stirring frequently, until the mixture thickens—about 10 minutes. Remove from the heat and cool.

Now, preheat the oven to 425° F. Roll out the pastry on a floured board until it is approximately ⅛ inch thick. Fit the crust into a greased 9-inch pie tin, and trim the edge to about ½ inch above the rim. Roll the overlapping pastry toward the outside. Flute the edges. Line the pastry with waxed paper and cover with a handful of dried beans. Prick the sides to let air escape. Bake 20 minutes and cool.

Stir the drained yogurt into the cooled berry mixture, and return to the refrigerator.

When both the berry filling and pie shell are cool, pour the chilled mixture into the chilled pie shell and refrigerate no more than 2 hours (otherwise the crust will become soggy).

Top with sweetened yogurt, whipped cream, or ice cream, if desired.

Yield: 6 to 8 servings.

Adapted from *Cooking with Yogurt.*

Lemon Cream Cheese Pie

Crust:

2 cups crushed graham crackers
¼ cup melted butter
2 tablespoons honey

Filling:

1 cup heavy cream
8 ounces cream cheese, softened
¼ cup honey
3 tablespoons lemon juice
Rind of half a lemon, grated

Combine the graham cracker crumbs, butter, and honey. Set aside 2 tablespoons of this mixture as a topping. Press the rest of the crust firmly on the sides and bottom of a 9-inch pie pan.

Whip the heavy cream and set aside. Whip the cream cheese until soft. Drizzle in the honey while mixing. Add the lemon juice and grated rind and blend. Fold the whipped cream into the cream cheese. Spoon the filling into the crust and top with the reserved crust mixture. Refrigerate at least 3 to 4 hours.

Serves 8.

Adapted from *Cooking with Honey.*

Squash Pie

Pastry for a 9-inch pie
Egg white
3½ cups cooked, mashed acorn squash
¼ cup honey
1 teaspoon salt
½ teaspoon cinnamon
½ teaspoon ginger
½ teaspoon nutmeg
1 egg
1¾ cups milk

Use your favorite recipe to make a single pie crust. Brush with a slightly beaten egg white. Preheat oven to 450° F.

Blend the rest of the ingredients together. Pour the filling into the pie shell and bake for 10 minutes at 450° F. Then reduce the heat to 300° F. and bake until firm, usually 45 to 50 minutes.

This rich pie serves 10.

Adapted from *Cooking with Honey*.

Rhubarb-Strawberry Pie

Two 9-inch pie crusts, unbaked
¾ cup brown sugar
½ cup white sugar
2 tablespoons flour
1 teaspoon lemon rind, grated
2 cups fresh strawberries, sliced
2 cups raw rhubarb, cut in ¼-inch pieces

Preheat oven to 375° F. Place one pie crust in pie pan. Combine brown sugar, white sugar, flour, and lemon rind. Toss lightly with fruit. Fill one pie shell. Cover with top crust. Bake 50 minutes.

Serves 8.

Adapted from *Great Rhubarb Recipes*.

Healthful Sugar Substitutes

Baking? If you have never used honey in baking, you will have a pleasant surprise. The moisture in honey will keep baked goods moist and fresh for a long time. It will soften cookie batters, which is fine for soft chewy-type cookies. But if the cookie is a crisp-type, just add 4 extra tablespoons of flour for each ¼ cup of honey used. Remember that honey caramelizes at a low temperature, so bake at a lower oven temperature. For cakes and other baked products for example, reduce the oven heat from 350° F. to 325° F. Avoid having the product brown well on the surface but be insufficiently baked in the interior.

Canning? Honey can replace all of the sugar generally used in canning, preserving, and jelly making. A syrup made from honey may be somewhat darker in color than a sugar syrup, and will tend to darken fruit such as peaches and pears. No matter. The honey will intensify the fruit flavor. Remember that honey has a tendency to foam considerably when it is heated. Use a large cooking kettle and watch the pot carefully to avoid having the syrup boil over. Also, since honey contains some liquid, it will be necessary to cook the product slightly longer than usual to evaporate this liquid.

You may wish to experiment with other natural sweeteners. If you use molasses as a substitute, follow the same rule as with honey and reduce the liquid in the recipe. Replace 1 cup of white sugar with 1 cup of unsulfured molasses, or with ¾ cup of unsulfured molasses plus ¼ cup of blackstrap molasses. Sorghum syrup is another good replacer. Use 1 cup of sorghum syrup for each cup of white sugar. If you use maple syrup, carob syrup, or malt syrup as replacers you may need to use slightly more, since these syrups are not quite as sweet as the others. Use 1¼ to 1½ cups of these syrups as replacers for each cup of white sugar.

Gradually reduce the amount of sweeteners used in baked goods, or over foods, and you can reduce your craving for the sweet taste. The palate adjusts, and you will find that a little bit of sweetening is satisfying.

Adapted from *Sugar & Sweeteners*.

Rosy Red Pie

2 pastry pie crusts, unbaked

1 tablespoon tapioca

1½ pounds rhubarb, cut into 1-inch lengths

¾ cup sugar

½ cup flour

¼ teaspoon salt

1 teaspoon lemon peel, grated

2 tablespoons butter or margarine

1 egg white, beaten

2 teaspoons sugar

Preheat oven to 450° F. Place one pie crust in pie pan and sprinkle tapioca over it. Combine rhubarb with sugar, flour, salt, and lemon peel. Mix well. Spoon mixture into pie shell. Dot pie with bits of butter. Cover rhubarb mixture with top crust. Brush pie with egg white and sprinkle with additional sugar. Bake 15 minutes at 450° F. Reduce to 375° F. and bake an additional 20 minutes until suitably brown.

Serves 8.

Adapted from *Great Rhubarb Recipes*.

Peach Vinegar Pie

Vinegar Pie goes way back in American history to the time when vanilla and lemon juice were difficult to obtain and vinegar was used as a substitute. Don't let the name "vinegar pie" scare you off. This is a fabulous dessert.

You could use raspberry or blueberry vinegar for this, too. The pie doesn't contain enough vinegar to give the strange color you might expect.

4 tablespoons butter or margarine

1 cup sugar

6 tablespoons flour

1 teaspoon mixed "pumpkin pie spice" (optional) — I find this unnecessary, but many of the pioneers added this much spice and more to their vinegar pies)

¼ cup peach, apricot or nectarine vinegar

2 eggs, lightly beaten

2 cups water

1 partially baked 9-inch pie shell

Cream the butter and sugar together, then stir in, in this order, the flour, spice mixture (if you're using it), vinegar, egg, and water. Put into a double boiler and cook until thickened, stirring frequently. Pour into the pie shell. Preheat oven to 350° F.

Bake for 35 minutes or until set, then allow to cool before serving.

Adapted from *Making & Using Flavored Vinegars*.

Except as noted, material in this chapter has been excerpted and adapted from Baking with Sourdough, *Storey/Garden Way Publishing Country Wisdom Bulletin A-50.*

CHAPTER 6

Sweet Temptations

Homemade Candies as Gifts

What's the very best present you can give to the traditional person who "has everything?" My vote goes to homemade candy. It's also the perfect present for almost any occasion that comes along, whether a birthday, Christmas, for a hostess gift, or as a "little something" for your child's teacher.

No one ever gets over a love for candy. We can go years without eating it — and decades without making it. But put a plateful of our own particular weakness (chocolate fudge, buttercrunch, caramel corn . . .) down beside us and see what happens: Strength of character disappears and so does the candy.

Long ago, candy-making was a social occasion. Notes were sent with such messages as, "Come to our house on Saturday — we're having a taffy pull." When was the last time you received an invitation of that sort? Never, I dare say. (Me, too.) Not many people make candy these days.

The candies you make are better in taste and quality than any you can buy. Just wait till you see how easy these are, how little working time they take, and how very inexpensive they are to make.

Before you start your candy-making, please read the section on ingredients and the one on taking your candy's temperature. This procedure is vital for the success of certain candies. There's even a brand-new shortcut way to do it.

Ingredients

I implore you to use pure, real vanilla, not artificial vanilla or vanillin. The difference in taste is unbelievable.

I also want to urge you to use only real chocolate. There are artificial "chocolate" chips and morsels out there; avoid them. Filled and molded chocolate candies require a special chocolate; it's discussed in the section on "Designer Chocolates." For other purposes, use the standard real chocolate (semisweet, chips or unsweetened) available in all grocery stores.

The choice between butter and margarine is up to you. It's fine to use margarine in such highly flavored candies as chocolate fudge, but butter is essential for the more delicate concoctions — vanilla buttercreams, for instance.

Avoid artificial food colors and flavorings as much as you can. There are pure extracts and natural food colors on the market; buy them and use them.

Temperatures

I try to avoid this whenever possible, but there are times when you simply have to take your candy's temperature.

Of the three ways to do this, by far the simplest is to cook your candy in an electric fryer-cooker. Mix the ingredients before plugging it in, then set the dial for the temperature you want. When the light goes out, you're there.

A more traditional way is to use a candy thermometer. (Check its accuracy by heating it in water — when the water boils, it should read 212° F.)

Or you can put a little of the mixture into some very cold water, form it into a ball with your fingers and check results as below:

Soft-ball stage	234° to 240° F.
Firm-ball stage	244° to 250° F.
Hard-ball stage	265° to 270° F.
Soft-crack stage	275° to 280° F.
Hard-crack stage	285° to 300° F.

Brittles

Brittles are very good, they are low-fat — and they're easy to make. All brittles should be made only when the weather is dry. They will keep better in airtight tins.

Peanut Brittle

Butter to grease a cookie sheet
1⅓ cups sugar
6½ ounce can "cocktail peanuts"

Before you start, butter a cookie sheet thoroughly.

Cook the sugar in a frying pan over low heat until it has melted and turned a light brown. Stir in the peanuts, then pour onto the baking sheet.

Now immediately start stretching the candy by pressing it out with the backs of two spoons. Don't touch it with your hands, as it will be very hot. Keep this up, working quickly, until the brittle is no more than 1 peanut deep.

When the candy is completely cool, break it into pieces. Keep in an airtight tin.

Other Nut Brittles

Substitute whatever nuts you want for the peanuts in peanut brittle, above. Salted nuts make the best-tasting brittles, and cashews are particularly good.

Caraway Comfits

This is my version of a confection that was very popular in eighteenth century England. It's supposed to be good for the digestion; it's also marvelous-tasting and a nice change from nut brittles.

Butter to grease a cookie sheet
1 cup sugar, granulated or raw
6 tablespoons caraway seeds

Before you start, butter a cookie sheet thoroughly.

Cook the sugar and caraway seeds together in a frying pan until the sugar has melted and is just beginning to turn color.

Pour onto the buttered cookie sheet and immediately start stretching it out with the backs of two spoons. Don't touch, since it will be very hot.

When candy is completely cool, break into brittle-sized pieces.

Blueberry Vinegar Candy

I've been making vinegar candy since I was a small child, and have always loved it. And it's even better made with Blueberry Vinegar. Besides, you can really startle people with blue candy. Raspberry Vinegar Candy's good, too. All are sweet-and-tangy.

2 tablespoons butter (plus more to grease a pan)
2 cups sugar
½ cup blueberry or raspberry vinegar (see page 66)

Grease a large pan or cookie sheet.

Melt the 2 tablespoons of butter in a saucepan, then add the sugar and vinegar. Stir over medium heat until the sugar has dissolved, then turn the heat up a bit and boil gently, stirring frequently, until the mixture reaches 300° F. (the hot end of the hard-crack stage). Pour onto the pan or cookie sheet.

For a vinegar taffy, cook only to 275° F., then pull.

Adapted from *Making & Using Flavored Vinegars.*

Burnt-Sugar Brittle

Use ingredients and directions as for Vinegar Candy, above. Cook until it reaches 325° F. or a strong brown color.

Benne Candy

Benne (pronounced benny) is sesame seed. It makes an outstanding candy.

1½ cups sesame seeds
Butter to grease a pan
2 cups sugar
1 teaspoon real vanilla

Spread the sesame seeds in a medium-sized pan and bake at 350° F. until toasted. (This takes just a few minutes; keep an eye on them to prevent burning.)

Butter a cookie sheet very thoroughly. Cook the sugar in a frying pan, stirring most of the time, until melted. Remove from the stove and very quickly stir in the vanilla and sesame seeds.

Pour onto the cookie sheet. When the candy has cooled a little, but is still warm, mark it into squares with a knife. When completely cool, break into squares.

Fudge

If you've had problems making a truly creamy chocolate fudge, this is the recipe for you:

Always-Creamy Chocolate Fudge

1 tablespoon butter or margarine (plus more to grease the pan)

6 ounces evaporated milk

2¼ cups sugar

One 12-ounce bag real chocolate semi-sweet chips

½ ounce unsweetened baking chocolate

3½ ounces marshmallow cream (half of a 7-ounce jar)

½ teaspoon real vanilla

½ cup broken walnuts or pecans (optional)

Combine the butter, sugar and evaporated milk in a saucepan. Bring to a rolling boil and cook for exactly 6 minutes.

In the meantime, grease a 10 x 10-inch pan, and put the chocolate chips, unsweetened chocolate and marshmallow cream in the large bowl of a mixer (or beat by hand).

At the end of the 6 minutes of furious boiling, pour the hot mixture over the ingredients in the bowl. Beat until smooth, then add the vanilla and the nuts. Pour into a greased pan to cool before cutting.

Since there's no such thing as too much chocolate fudge, you might want to multiply all of the ingredients by three and use a large jelly-roll pan.

Brown Sugar Fudge

Also known as penuche, panocha, ponoche, etc.

2 cups granulated sugar

2 cups brown sugar

1 cup heavy cream

2 tablespoons butter (plus more to grease a pan)

¼ cup water

1 cup broken walnuts or pecans (optional)

Butter a roughly 10 x 10-inch pan.

Put all the ingredients except the nuts in a large saucepan. Bring to a boil, stirring only until the butter and sugars have melted. Cook at a rolling boil for exactly 5 minutes.

Beat until the mixture is thick and lighter in color and has lost its gloss.

Stir in the nuts and spoon into the buttered pan.

Allow to cool thoroughly before cutting into small squares.

Vanilla Fudge

A very white and creamy variation.

2 tablespoons butter (plus more for
    greasing a pan)
3 cups sugar
1½ cups half-and-half
¼ cup corn syrup
1 tablespoon vanilla
1 cup broken walnuts or pecans (optional)

Grease a roughly 8 x 8-inch pan.

Combine the butter, sugar, half-and-half and corn syrup in a medium-sized saucepan. Stir until it comes to a boil, then continue cooking, stirring only from time to time, until it reaches 235° F. (the soft-ball stage).

Remove from the heat. When cool enough to touch comfortably, add the vanilla, transfer to the bowl of a mixer and beat until the mixture has thickened and lost its gloss. Stir in the nuts and spoon into the buttered pan. Cut into squares when thoroughly cool.

Caramels

Caramels are among America's favorite candies. However, they are adversely affected by moisture in the air, so you have to wrap each little candy in plastic wrap.

Vanilla Caramels

A rather hard caramel, which softens slightly after it's wrapped in plastic or encased in chocolate.

2 cups sugar
½ cup corn syrup
1½ cups medium cream
4 tablespoons butter (plus more for
    greasing a baking pan)
1¼ teaspoons vanilla

Cook the sugar, corn syrup, cream and the 4 tablespoons of butter in a medium-sized saucepan, stirring often, to the firm-ball stage (246° F.).

Remove from the stove and stir in the vanilla. Pour onto a well-buttered marble slab or baking tin.

When thoroughly cold, cut into small squares and wrap.

Coffee Caramels

1 cup sugar
1 cup light corn syrup
1 cup evaporated milk
¼ cup double-strength coffee (can be
    decaffeinated)
4 ounces butter (plus more for greasing a
    baking pan)
½ teaspoon vanilla

Cook the sugar and the corn syrup in a medium-size saucepan to the firm-ball stage (246° F.), stirring often. Combine the evaporated milk and coffee and add, along with small pieces of the butter, to the hot mixture. (Add very slowly so the boiling won't stop.) Keep boiling, stirring constantly, until the mixture is back at 246° F. (the firm-ball stage).

Remove from the fire, stir in the vanilla and pour into a well-buttered baking pan. When thoroughly cold, turn out of the pan, cut into squares and wrap.

Designer Filled Chocolates

When you want to give a magnificent present to someone, make these wonderfully sinful candies. Most people will think they've been hand-dipped, but they're made in special molds that produce a glossy, highly professional-looking candy.

Go to a candy-making supply store, or a cake decorating supply store. You'll need coating chocolate, and (reusable) candy molds.

Disks of coating chocolate come in one-pound bags, either dark (semisweet)

or milk chocolate (very sweet). Use only coating chocolate for molding unless you're already a pro. Other varieties require "tempering" by an elaborate, several-step, temperature-controlled process.

Basic Buttercream Filling

(Also known as Uncooked Fondant)
Use this filling, just as it is, to make vanilla buttercreams. Add other ingredients to it to make a wide variety of buttercreams (see below).

⅓ cup butter, at room temperature
⅓ cup white corn syrup
1½ teaspoons real vanilla
3 cups confectioners' sugar

Combine all the ingredients. The mixture will keep, well wrapped and refrigerated, for weeks and weeks.

General Directions for Filled Chocolates

First, assemble the things you'll need:

- Disks of coating chocolate (preferably dark)

- A small jar (an 8-ounce screwtop Mason-type jar is ideal)

- A small saucepan half-filled with hot (but never, at any point, boiling) water

- A small spoon

- Plastic candy molds (one for each sort of candy you want to make)

- Filling

- Waxed paper

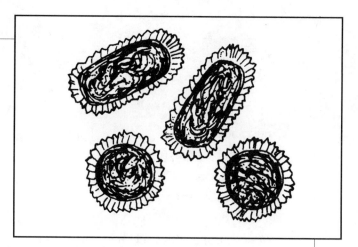

Put enough coating chocolate disks into the small jar to fill it about halfway. Place this in the pan of hot, but not boiling, water. (Don't let any water get into the jar.)

When the wafers are melted, stir well. Then, using the small spoon, put a little chocolate in each of the depressions in the candy mold, coating each depression thoroughly, but thinly. Place in your freezer until firm — about 15 minutes.

Now place a small ball of filling in each little chocolate-coated hole. Press it in gently so it's level, then top with a thin layer of melted chocolate, making sure that the filling is completely enclosed by chocolate. Put back in the freezer for another few minutes, or until the chocolate on top is firm.

Unmold by holding the candy mold upside down about an inch over a sheet of waxed paper. Gently flex the mold and the beautiful, shiny little candies will pop right out. (If by chance they don't, just freeze a bit more.)

As you need it, add more wafers to the jar of chocolate, stirring as they melt. When your candymaking session is over, cool the chocolate in the jar to room temperature. Close it tightly and keep it, still at room temperature, ready for the next time.

Non-Designer Filled Chocolates

Use any of the buttercream filling variations below (except liquid cherries). Form it into small balls, then dip these into melted regular chocolate (unsweetened is spectacular; semi-sweet is also excellent),

turning to coat all sides. Put on waxed paper to set.

Other Buttercreams

In each case, start with ½ cup of the basic buttercream filling, which will make approximately 2 to 3 dozen buttercreams, depending on the size of the mold you use. (The fairly large "bonbon" molds each use about a teaspoon of filling.)

Flavor the ½ cup of filling as suggested below, then follow the general directions for filled chocolates, above.

Coffee Buttercreams

Add ¾ teaspoon instant coffee powder.

Chocolate Buttercreams

Add 2 tablespoons melted coating chocolate.

Coconut Buttercreams

Add 2 tablespoons grated coconut. (Optional: a few drops of coconut flavor extract.)

Maple-Walnut Buttercreams

Add 2 tablespoons finely minced

walnuts and ¼ teaspoon maple flavoring extract.

Lemon, Orange, Lime, Mint, or Wintergreen Buttercreams

Add a few drops of flavor extract to taste, plus a little food coloring. Make fancy mints in a mint patty mold.

Almond Buttercreams

Either add a few drops of almond extract to the basic buttercream filling, or use little balls of marzipan.

Chocolate-Covered Liquid Cherries

Use a candy mold with extra-large depressions. Line each depression in the mold with chocolate and freeze briefly.

Maraschino cherries and their juice
Basic buttercream filling
Coating chocolate

Now put a cherry (or half of one) into each chocolate-lined hole. Stir enough maraschino cherry juice into some basic buttercream filling to make a consistency a little softer than mayonnaise. Put a very small amount of this on top of each cherry.

Cover each candy with a layer of coating chocolate, making extra-sure that you've sealed the filling. Freeze for about 15 minutes — then turn out onto waxed paper.

The centers will start to liquefy in about two hours, but will be at their best after two days.

Liquid Cherries with Kirsch or Other Liqueurs

Follow the recipe above for Liquid Cherries, but use kirsch or another liqueur (perhaps an orange-flavored one) instead of maraschino juice to thin down the buttercream filling.

Other Filled and Dipped Candies

Chocolate-Covered Fudge

These give quite a different effect from the chocolate buttercreams above. Just cook and cool any of the fudges from this bulletin. Form the fudge into small balls and use these exactly as you would buttercream filling.

Candied Orange Peel

This is a simplified, but superb, candied orange peel. The only way you can improve it is to coat it with chocolate (see below).

2 large navel oranges
½ cup sugar
¼ cup water
1 tablespoon light corn syrup
Extra sugar for rolling (optional)

Peel the oranges in long lengthwise strips. Simmer with enough water to cover until the orange peel is tender.

Drain off the water and let the peel cool. Scrape away the white part. Cut the peel into strips about ¼-inch wide.

Put into a saucepan with the sugar, water, and corn syrup. Cook over low heat until clear (230° F.). Drain in a colander over a bowl (save the syrup to add to cakes, cookies or iced tea).

When cool, roll the strips in sugar if you're not planning to coat them with chocolate.

Chocolate-Coated Candied Orange Peel

Use candied orange peel (above), *not* rolled in extra sugar. Dip the entire piece of fruit. Put on waxed paper to set.

Marzipan

Marzipan can bring out the artist in you. No other sort of candymaking is quite as much fun as shaping your marzipan mixture into tiny fruits, vegetables, eggs, or even flowers.

You can buy prepared marzipan in almost any supermarket. Making your own, though, isn't hard to do and is better in every way, including cost.

Basic Marzipan Mixture

1 cup blanched almonds
2 cups confectioners' sugar
½ teaspoon almond extract
2 egg whites, lightly beaten

Grind the almonds very fine by putting them through a meat grinder three or four times, or by running them in a blender or food processor, being sure to stop the machine before you've created almond butter. Add the confectioners' sugar and almond extract, then mix in the egg white a teaspoon at a time, using just enough to make a nice claylike mixture.

General Instructions for Marzipan

Roll the marzipan into small balls, then create the objects you want. To color marzipan, you can work food coloring into the marzipan itself before shaping; or let the shapes dry an hour then, using an artist's brush, paint them with food colorings. To dilute a color, add water.

Make your shapes all about the same size. Thus strawberries will be more or less life-size, but oranges and lemons will be smaller than real fruits.

Other Marzipan Possibilities

Other shapes you can make include apples, pears, bananas, potatoes, peaches (make a deep groove down each side of the fruit), carrots, purpletop turnips, peas in the pod (just one side of a pod, open, filled with six or seven peas), corn on the cob (use a toothpick to mark the rows of kernels), etc.

Chocolate-Coated Marzipan

Chocolate and marzipan make one of the world's great combinations. See the general instructions for filled chocolates, substituting marzipan for the buttercream filling.

For larger candies, make little finger-sized logs of marzipan and dip them in chocolate.

Truffles

Truffles are the chocoholic's favorite. Luckily, they're easy and comparatively inexpensive to make. No one has ever accused them of being low-calorie, though.

Keep the cream-based truffles refrigerated or frozen. If you wish to ship truffles to a friend, use Kentucky bourbon balls or other variations of cookie-based candies.

Basic Mixture for Truffles

¼ cup heavy cream
6 tablespoons cocoa
12 ounces real chocolate chips
6 tablespoons butter, at room temperature (soft)
1 teaspoon real vanilla

Combine the cream, cocoa and chocolate chips in a small saucepan. Stir over very low heat until the chocolate has melted. Remove from the fire and stir in first the vanilla, then the soft butter.

Chill until firm enough to work with, then form into whatever size balls you wish. Truffles may be rolled in dry cocoa, or dipped in chocolate, either dark or white. Place on waxed paper until set.

Liqueur Truffles

Follow the basic truffle recipe, but instead of vanilla, add 1 tablespoon of Grand Marnier, Amaretto, Kahlua, or any other liqueur.

Mint-Chocolate Truffles

To the basic recipe for truffles, add, instead of the vanilla, either 1 tablespoon of crème de menthe or a few drops of mint flavor extract.

Kentucky Bourbon Balls

These were around long before the name "truffle" began to be applied to candies. They're terrific — but not to be fed to children.

1 cup confectioners' sugar
3 tablespoons cocoa powder
2 tablespoons light corn syrup
¼ cup bourbon
3 cups crushed vanilla wafers
More confectioners' sugar and/or cocoa
    powder for coating

Stir the confectioners' sugar and the cocoa powder together in a medium-sized bowl. Mix the corn syrup and bourbon together and stir into the dry mixture. Now add the crushed vanilla wafers and combine very thoroughly.

Form into one-inch or larger balls. Roll in confectioners' sugar, cocoa, or a combination, and put on a rack to dry. Coat again, if you wish, after half an hour.

Chocolate-Rum Balls

Substitute dark rum for the bourbon in Kentucky Bourbon Balls.

Chocolate-Orange-Ginger Balls

Here's a variation that children can have fun making and eating. Follow the Kentucky Bourbon Ball recipe, substituting orange juice for the bourbon and ginger snaps for the vanilla wafers.

Taffy

How to Pull Taffy

Let your cooked taffy sit just until barely cool enough to work with. (If it gets too cool, you can warm it in a 350° F. oven for 3 or 4 minutes.) Form it into one or more balls. Now start pulling:

Use just your fingertips and thumbs, well-coated with cornstarch or butter.

Working fast, pull a lump of the candy between the fingertips of one hand and the other until it's about 15 inches long. Now double it up and pull again. Repeat until the candy is porous and hard to pull.

Stretch into a rope about ¾ inch in diameter. Cut with greased scissors into 1-inch pieces. Wrap in waxed paper. Keep wrapped taffies in a tightly closed tin.

Molasses Taffy

2 cups unsulfured molasses
1 cup sugar
2 tablespoons cider or white vinegar
2 tablespoons butter (plus more to grease
    a pan)

Combine all the ingredients in a large saucepan. Stir while bringing to a boil and cooking to 265° F. (the hard-ball stage). Pour onto a buttered platter or baking tin. Using a spatula, turn the edges toward the center to speed cooling. Pull.

Salt Water Taffy

2 cups sugar
¾ cup water
¼ cup corn syrup
1 teaspoon salt
Butter to grease a large pan or platter
Flavoring and coloring (see below)

Combine the sugar, water, corn syrup, and salt in a large saucepan. Stir until the sugar has dissolved, then boil to 265° F. (the hard-ball stage). Pour onto the platter or pan. Turn the edges toward the center with a spatula. Pull.

Add whatever flavoring and colorings you wish to use as you pull. For this size batch, use 1 teaspoon vanilla or other extract or ¼ teaspoon flavoring oil (available at pharmacies) and about 3 drops of food color.

Miscellaneous Candies

Peanut Butter Fondant

A different and delicious candy that requires no cooking.

½ cup peanut butter
1 cup dry powdered milk
½ cup honey
¾ cup coconut or crushed nuts (optional)

Combine all of the ingredients in a bowl and stir until well blended. Pat it into a buttered 8 x 8-inch pan, chill, and cut into squares. Or make the dough into small balls and roll into coconut or crushed nuts, then chill. This candy could also be chocolate-coated.

Adapted from *Cooking with Honey.*

Butterscotch

This is a light butterscotch. If you'd like it darker, substitute 1 cup brown sugar for 1 cup of the granulated, and molasses for the corn syrup.

2 cups granulated sugar
⅔ cup corn syrup
½ cup half-and-half
4 tablespoons butter (plus more to grease both a saucepan and a cooling pan)

Grease a 9 x 9-inch baking tin and the top few inches of a medium-sized saucepan.

Combine the sugar, corn syrup and half-and-half in the saucepan. Cook until it reaches 260° F. (the hard-ball stage). Stir in the butter, 1 tablespoon at a time, and continue boiling, stirring constantly, to 280° F. (the soft-crack stage).

Pour into the pan. When cool enough to touch comfortably, mark into small squares. When cold, break apart.

Pralines

From the Deep South. Pralines keep best when wrapped individually.

2 cups light brown sugar
1 cup cream
1 cup pecan halves
½ teaspoon vanilla

Combine the brown sugar and cream in a large saucepan. Stir until the sugar is melted, then boil to 236° F. (the soft-ball stage).

Remove from the fire and stir in the vanilla and pecans. Stir until the mixture begins to thicken and turn sugary. (The best test for this is to taste some of it.) Drop from a large spoon onto waxed paper, pressing each mound of candy out as best you can. Wrap when cool.

Grease a large baking sheet.

Melt the half-pound of butter with the sugar in a medium-sized saucepan. Boil, stirring, until a candy thermometer registers 285° F. (the hard-crack stage), then stir in the vanilla and quickly pour the mixture onto the baking sheet.

Melt the chocolate and the 1 tablespoon of butter over very low heat or in a double boiler. Spread half of this over the candy on the baking sheet, then sprinkle on half the almonds. Press them in lightly.

Put in your refrigerator until thoroughly hardened, then turn the whole thing over, spread with the remaining chocolate (melted again if it has hardened) and sprinkle on and press in the rest of the almonds. Refrigerate again until hard, then break into fairly small pieces.

Except as noted, material in this chapter has been excerpted and adapted from Making Homemade Candy, *Storey/Garden Way Publishing Country Wisdom Bulletin A-111.*

Buttercrunch (English Toffee)

½ pound plus 1 tablespoon butter or margarine (plus more to grease a baking sheet)
1½ cups sugar
½ teaspoon vanilla
One 12-ounce package real semi-sweet chocolate chips
1 cup ground or thinly sliced nonblanched almonds

CHAPTER **7**

Gifts of Light

Making Your Own Soaps and Candles

The art of making soap and candles so closely follows the history of our country that we can almost read the character of the times and the people by asking what they did with surplus animal fats.

The first colonists brought their soap kettles with them and at butchering time made soap and candles in groups of families for all to share. As civilization crept in and the cities and towns developed, butchering was taken over by those who were paid for the task. Families put away their soap kettles and bought the hard yellow bars at the store along with the family food staples. The candles were replaced by kerosene and then electricity.

But many homesteaders and rural families — those that took pride in independence and abhorred waste — made their own soap well into the 20th century.

Then during World War II, when animal fat was used to the utmost and commercial soap was in short supply, many American women looked up

Grandmother's old recipes and revived the art of making soap and candles, this time on modern kitchen stoves.

And now we have come full circle, sharing the old concern for the land, and finding pleasure in preserving these almost-forgotten arts.

To yesterday's homesteader, animal fat was an important by-product of butchering. He raised his own meat and butchered it himself, saving every scrap of the animal for home use. The meat was dried and cured and canned. The hide was tanned. The head and intestines were saved for sausage. The fat was used for cooking and for making soap and candles.

From even a small, fairly lean calf a butcher trims and discards 50 to 100 pounds of fat, which could be rendered into a pure white, hard tallow. Larger, fatter animals will provide even more. This tallow can be converted into enough soap to last a family until the next butchering time. It also may be used to make candles. We've included recipes for both.

Different kinds of leftover kitchen grease can be used for soap-making. Even strong-smelling or rancid grease will make

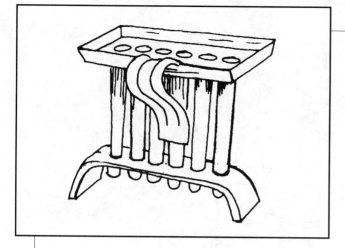

perfectly good, sweet-smelling soap.

Candles require clean, hard fat — preferably beef tallow which produces a harder, cleaner-smelling candle. Properly made homemade candles have no offensive odor.

Many of the enclosed recipes are one to two centuries old. To preserve their character we have retained the original wording as much as possible.

Some of the methods no longer may be practical and some of the ingredients may not be available. Wherever possible, we have clarified terms and simplified methods. You may need to substitute or improvise in some cases.

A few modern recipes such as Simple Kitchen Soap and Boiled Kitchen Soap have been included.

Making Soap

Making soap is one of the few ways a person with no special talent literally can "make something out of nothing." It also is a thrifty way to make good use of an otherwise wasted by-product of meat.

With a few simple kitchen tools, ingredients you probably already have on hand, and a few hours' work, you can make a month's supply of soap. It's a good idea to make soap once or twice a year because soap, like wine, improves with age.

The simplest and cheapest type is plain yellow laundry soap, the kind that made Grandmother's sheets so sparkling white. But with the addition of a few inexpensive ingredients you can create fine toilet soaps too.

The additional ingredients are used to make soap clean better, to soften the water or to perfume the product. Most of them are available at grocery or drug stores. A few, such as the essences and oils used in scented toilet soaps, can be purchased in hobby shops which carry supplies for making soaps and candles.

Powdered borax is sold in grocery stores as a water softener. Potash lye is on the same shelf labeled "drain cleaner." Quicklime or ground limestone may be found in garden supply shops. Most drug stores carry resin or will order it for you.

The instructions are simple. Try making your own soap. You'll find it's fun, but be careful.

Caution!!!

- Commercial lyes, potash lye, and soda lye — even dampened wood ashes — are **EXTREMELY** caustic and can cause burns if splashed on the skin. They could cause blindness if spattered in the eye.

- Use caution when adding lye to cold water, when stirring lye water and when pouring the liquid soap into molds. If it is spilled on the skin, wash off immediately with cold water. Wash off any lye or green (uncured) soap spilled on furniture or counter tops.

- Always add lye to **COLD** water, never to hot water, because the chemical action heats the cold water to the boiling point. It also produces harsh fumes which are harmful if breathed deeply. Stand back and avert the head while the lye is dissolving. Use a draft vent if possible.

- Dispose of soap-making wastes carefully outdoors, not in the drain. Never put lye or fresh soap in aluminum pans. Keep small children from the room while soap is being made.

You'll Need

A container — For large quantities, use a large iron soap kettle or a common wash boiler. For indoor soapmaking in smaller quantities, granite or porcelain-covered pots are best because of the corrosive character of some ingredients.

A long-handled wooden ladle or wooden spoon to stir the soap.

A grater or grinder — A kitchen grater or a meat grinder is needed to make soap flakes for laundry use or to grind soap for some recipes.

Molds — Grandmother used flat wooden boxes to mold the soap while it cooled and hardened. Over the wood she laid pieces of cloth to keep the soap from sticking to the wood. You can buy fancy molds in hobby shops, but for home use discarded plastic bottles work just as well.

A plate on which to test a few drops of the liquid for doneness. A glass plate cools the liquid faster.

The Ingredients

There are only three ingredients in plain soap — animal fat, lye and water. All three can be obtained free. Unwanted fat scraps often are free for the asking at butcher shops or butchering plants. Just tell them what you want it for. A few hours over low heat (wood for an outdoor fire often is free for the chopping) and you have all the fat needed for a year's supply of soap.

And save the ashes from that fire. You'll need them to make the lye — also free. For recipes that call for soft water use rain water, chemically softened water or borax added to tap water.

To Prepare Tallow or Grease

Cut up beef suet, mutton tallow or pork scraps and fry over low heat. Strain the melted grease through a coarse cloth and squeeze as much grease as possible out of the scraps. If you have an old lard press, it was made for this step.

Now clean the melted fat by boiling it in water to which a tablespoon of salt or alum has been added. Add twice as much water as fat and boil 10 minutes. Stir thoroughly and allow to cool. When the fat is cold it will have formed a hard cake on top of the water. Lift off the cake of fat and scrape the underside clean. Weigh and melt down according to the recipe.

To Make Potash Lye from Ashes

For a small quantity, use a porcelain-covered or plastic pail. Fill the pail with ashes and add boiling water, stirring to wet the ashes. The ashes will settle to less than one-fourth their original volume. Add ashes to the top of the pail, stir again and let stand for 12 to 24 hours, or until the liquid is clear. Then carefully pour, dip, or siphon off the clear liquid.

The strength of the lye need not always be the same, since in the soap-making the alkali will unite only with a certain proportion of fat, and more lye can be added until all the fat is saponified. Lye that will float a fresh egg is standard strength for soap-making.

A Glossary of Ingredients

- **Lye, Lye Water, and Potash Lye** (sometimes termed **Caustic Potash Lye**) are made from steeped (slaked) wood ashes and are interchangeable terms.

- **Potash** (sometimes called **Caustic Potash**) is lye water evaporated to a powder.

- **Lime** (or **Stone Lime**) is ground or agricultural limestone.

- **Quicklime** is lime that has been baked.

- **Soda Lye** is quicklime slaked in water and heated with sal soda.

- **Sal Soda** is hydrated sodium carbonate.

- **Caustic Soda** is soda lye evaporated to a powder.

- **Commercial Lye** usually is the same as caustic soda and is the equivalent of "lye" in most recipes.

To Make Potash

Potash may be made by boiling down the lye water in a heavy iron kettle. After the water is driven off there will remain a dark, dry residue which is known as "black salts." The heat must be maintained until this is melted, when the black impurities will be burned away and a grayish-white substance will remain. This is potash. Save what you don't use for the next time you make soap.

To Make Soda Lye

Slake 1 quart of quicklime with 3 quarts water, which will reduce the lime to the consistency of cream. Dissolve 3 quarts sal soda in 5 quarts boiling water. Add the slaked lime, stirring vigorously. Keep the mixture at a boil until the ingredients are thoroughly mixed.

Allow the mixture to cool and settle, then pour off the lye liquid and discard the dregs in the bottom. Caustic soda may be produced from this liquid by boiling down the lye until the water is evaporated, and a dry residue is left in the kettle.

Commercial Lye

Most commercial lyes are caustic soda. One can of commercial lye may be substituted for the one pound of lye called for in most of the following recipes.

The Methods

To make any soap it is necessary to dilute lye, then mix it with fat or oil and stir until saponification takes place.

Saponification is the chemical reaction by which the two ingredients — lye water and fat — are converted into one substance — soap.

Soft soaps have saponified when they are thick and creamy, with a slightly slimy texture. They do not harden and are ready to use at this stage.

Uncooked hard soaps are ready to be poured into molds when the emulsion has thickened to the consistency of honey. Boiled hard soaps have saponified when the mixture is thick and ropy and slides off the spoon.

If lye water and fat are mixed when they are cold, the process of saponification may require several days or even months, depending upon the strength and purity of the ingredients. But if the temperature is raised to 212° F., the process of saponification will take place in a few minutes or few hours.

These are the two methods of making soap: the cold process and the boiling process. We've included both methods in the recipes for hard soap.

Hard Soap

The old-fashioned boiling method of making hard soap requires three kettles — two small kettles to hold the lye and the fat respectively, and one large enough to contain both ingredients without boiling over.

Put the clean fat or grease in one of the smaller kettles with enough water or weak lye to prevent burning, and raise the temperature to a boil. Put the lye water or a solution of sal soda or potash or both in the other small kettle and dissolve in boiling water.

Place the kettle on the fire and ladle into it about one-fourth of the melted fat. Add an equal quantity of the hot lye, stirring the mixture constantly. Continue this way, one person ladling and another stirring, until about two-thirds of the fat and lye have been mixed thoroughly together.

At this stage the mixture should be a uniform emulsion of about the consistency of cream. A few drops of fluid cooled on a glass plate should show neither globules of oil nor water separately.

Now add enough strong lye to complete the decomposition of the fats and the removal of the glycerin. Continue boiling until the mixture has a strong alkaline or burning taste. *NOTE: We do not recommend that you taste soap.* Add the remainder of the fat and lye alternately, taking care that in the end there shall be no excess lye. Evaporate the excess water by boiling down.

At this point add salt. This breaks up the creamy emulsion of oils and alkali. The salt takes the water and causes the soap to separate and rise on the surface of the lye in a curdy, granulated state. The mother liquid or spent lye will contain glycerin, salt and other impurities, but no fat or alkali. Skim off the soap.

To Improve Hard Soap

A better quality soap may be made by remelting the product of the first boiling and adding more fats or oils and lye as needed until the mixture has a decided taste of alkali (see *NOTE* above). Then

boil the whole until saponification is complete.

If pure grained fat and good white lye are used the resulting product will be a pure, white, hard soap that will be suitable for all household purposes. The time required for this final step will depend on the strength of the lye, but usually from two to four hours of boiling is necessary.

To Pack and Preserve Hard Soap

When hard soap has saponified pour the honey-thick mixture into molds or shallow wooden boxes, over which loose pieces of cloth have been placed to keep the soap from sticking. Or soap may be cooled and solidified by pouring it into a wooden washtub or firkin which has been soaked overnight in water. Do not use aluminum. Cover with towels or a throw rug to keep the heat in. Let set two to three days.

When cold the soap may be cut into small bars with a smooth, hard cord or a fine wire. A knife may be used but it chips the soap. Now pack the bars loosely, corncob fashion, so air will circulate freely, on slat shelves in a cool, dry place to season and become thoroughly dry and hard.

Be careful! Uncured or "green" soap is almost as caustic as wet lye. Wear rubber gloves when handling the hardened soap until it has been aged a few weeks.

Hard Soap Recipes

To make this soap, melt the fat over low heat, then add it to the cooled lye water in a heavy crock. No cooking is required.

Simple Kitchen Soap

Dissolve 1 can commercial lye in 5 cups cold water. The union of lye and water generates great heat, so be careful not to splash it on your skin. Stir until dissolved. Cool to 80° F. Meanwhile mix 2 tablespoons each powdered borax and liquid ammonia in ½ cup water. Melt 6 pounds clarified grease, strain and cool to body temperature. Pour the warm grease into the lye water and beat the mass with an egg beater, gradually adding the borax and ammonia mixture. Stir until a complete emulsion is formed, about 10 to 15 minutes. Pour into a mold to cool. *OR:*

Melt 5½ pounds grease and strain through a coarse cloth. Allow the grease to cool, but before it hardens add 1 can commercial lye dissolved in 3 pints cold water. Stir vigorously until the mixture thickens. Let stand five to six days in molds.

Boiled Hard White Soap

Dissolve 1 pound potash lye in 1 gallon cold water. Let mixture stand overnight, then pour the clear liquid into a second gallon of boiling water and bring it to a boil. Pour in a thin stream 4 pounds melted fat heated to the boiling point. Stir constantly until an emulsion is formed. Simmer four to six hours, then add another gallon of hot water in which is dissolved 1 cup salt. To test for doneness, lift some of the mixture on a cold knife blade. If it is ropy and clear and cools quickly, the mixture is saponified. This makes about 25 pounds white soap.

Boiled Kitchen Soap

Dissolve 2½ pounds commercial lye in 5 quarts cold water, stirring carefully so as not to splash. Cool slightly, then add 10 pounds tallow. Bring to a boil over low heat and boil, stirring, until it saponifies. Pour into molds and let set one week before turning out. This soap should be aged three to four weeks before using. It is best after several months.

Babbit's Premium Soap

To make about 100 pounds of soap, mix 5 gallons lye water in 5 gallons soft water and bring to a boil. Boil ½ hour. Then add 5 pounds tallow, 1 pound potash, 2 pounds sal soda, ½ pound resin, 1 pint salt and 1 pint ammonia. Boil until it saponifies, stirring constantly. Pour into molds.

Testing Soaps

To test soap for doneness take out a little and allow to cool. If no grease rises to the top and liquid hardens, it is done. If grease rises add lye and boil longer.

English Bar Soap

Take 1 gallon soft water, 1 pound stone (ground or agricultural) lime, 3¼ pounds sal soda, 1 ounce borax, 2½ pounds tallow, 1¾ pounds pulverized rosin and 1 ounce beeswax. Bring the water to a boil, then gradually add the lime and soda, stirring vigorously. Add the borax. Boil and stir until dissolved. Pour in the melted tallow in a thin stream, stirring constantly. Add the rosin and beeswax. Boil and stir until it thickens. Cool in molds.

Transparent Soap

Any good white neutral (neither alkaline nor acid) soap may be made transparent by reducing it to shavings, adding one-half its volume of alcohol and setting the mixture in a warm place until the soap is dissolved. When allowed to cool, the soap has somewhat the appearance of rock candy. It may be perfumed as desired. *OR*

Shave 24 ounces good hard yellow soap and add 1 pint of alcohol. Simmer in double boiler over low heat until dissolved. Remove from heat and add 1 ounce almond essence. Beat with an egg beater to make an emulsion. Pour into molds to cool.

Honey Soap

Shave and melt in a double boiler 2 pounds yellow soap. Add 4 ounces palm oil, 4 ounces honey and 1 ounce oil of cinnamon or other perfume. Boil 10 minutes. While cooling stir vigorously with an egg beater to emulsify ingredients. Cool. It is ready for use as soon as hardened.

Borax Soap

Dissolve 3 ounces borax in 2 quarts boiling water. Shave 2 pounds pure white hard soap and add. Stir and simmer over low heat until ingredients are thoroughly melted and mixed. When cold, soap is ready for use.

Oatmeal or Cornmeal Soaps

Grandmother believed oatmeal and cornmeal made the skin smooth, soft, and white. In summer she mixed 2 cups cornmeal with 2 tablespoons powdered borax and used it as a skin cleanser.

Perfumed Soaps

Soaps may be perfumed by adding a few drops of any essential oil or a proportionately larger quantity of essences or perfumed distilled waters to the saponified mass while cooling, but before hard soap has become cool enough to set. If perfumes are added while the soap is too hot they tend to volatilize and escape with the steam. If the soap is too cold they cannot be readily incorporated.

Perfumed Soap Recipes

Sandalwood Soap

To 7 pounds neutral soap add 2 ounces attar of bergamot and 7 ounces attar of sandalwood.

Rose Soap

To 30 pounds castile soap add 20 pounds tallow soap. Melt in enough water to keep from sticking. Add 3 ounces attar of rose, 1 ounce essence of cinnamon, 2½ ounces essence of bergamot, 1½ ounces vermilion and 1 ounce essence of cloves.

Bouquet Soap

Sliver 30 pounds tallow soap and melt in 2 cups water. When cooled add 4 ounces essence of bergamot, 1 ounce each of oils of cloves, sassafras, and thyme. Pour into molds.

Cinnamon Soap

Shave 50 pounds tallow soap and melt over low heat in 1 quart water. Cool. Add 7 ounces oil of cinnamon and 1 ounce each of essence of sassafras and bergamot. Mix. Add 1 pound finely powdered yellow ochre. Mix well and pour into molds.

Medicated Soaps

Many of these recipes are oddities today; some ingredients are rarely found.

Camphor Soap

Dissolve 1 pound neutral hard white soap in 1 cup boiling water. Continue boiling over low heat until soap is the consistency of butter. Add 6 ounces olive oil mixed with 1 ounce camphorated oil. Take from heat and beat with egg beater until a complete emulsion forms. Use to clean scratches.

Juniper Tar Soap

Dissolve 4 ounces tar in 1 pound almond oil or olive oil. Heat in double boiler and gradually add weak soda lye, stirring constantly until saponification takes place. This soap is to be applied at night and washed away next morning.

Making Candles

Americans always have loved candles, and with good reason. They are self-contained, cheap and portable. They make welcome gifts, help decorate the home and lend a romantic, elegant touch to the dinner table.

They're also very easy to make at home. You don't need an expensive kit, fancy molds or even special wicks. You still can make candles the way your great-grandmother made them — with what you have on hand. Here's how.

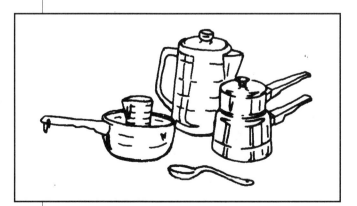

You'll Need

A Container — for melting the wax, tallow or paraffin. You'll need one large enough to hold a batch and heavy enough to keep it from burning. A kettle with a pouring spout is handy and A DOUBLE BOILER ARRANGEMENT FOR THE POTS IS ESSENTIAL FOR SAFETY. A large, restaurant-size tin can bent on one side to form a spout and placed in a large deep pan with an inch or two of water is one good, cheap solution.

Cheesecloth — for straining.

Long-Handled Spoon — long enough to reach the bottom of the container. Metal is best.

Molds — available in your kitchen or at the town dump. See "To Mold Candles".

Wicks — cotton string, cord or whatever you have on hand.

Tallow, Wax, or Paraffin — tallow is free, wax is expensive and paraffin is about $1.00 a pound. Take your pick.

The Methods

Homemade candles can be made from tallow (the hard fat of beef or mutton), from stearin (which is derived from tallow), from wax or paraffin.

Paraffin candles usually are molded; tallow candles may be dipped or molded; wax candles usually are rolled.

Molded Candles — Molds may be anything you have on hand, from a flat ashtray to a tall milk carton. There is no required shape for a candle. You can be as imaginative as you like with molds. If you simply need a light, pour your candle in a cup and carry it by the cup handle. Make it as simple or as elaborate as you wish.

Dipped Candles — The real, old-fashioned kind the Pilgrims made take more time but are much more traditional. They're made by dipping wicks, singly or several at a time on a frame, in hot wax or tallow. The wicks are immersed in the melted substance, removed to cool and dipped again and again to add one layer at a time until the candle is thick enough.

Rolled Candles — Rolled candles are made by pouring melted wax on the wicks in a thin layer, allowing it to partially set, then rolling the wax around the wick by hand while the wax is still warm.

Making the Wick

The first step in making the candle is to make the wick. Twist or braid together any kind of cotton string or cord to make the wick thick enough for the candle. Then soak in *one* of the following:

1. Turpentine.

2. Two ounces borax, 1 ounce chloride of lime, 1 ounce chloride of ammonia and 1 ounce saltpeter, dissolved in 3 quarts water.

3. One-half pound lime and 2 ounces saltpeter dissolved in 1 gallon of water.

Soak wicks 15 to 20 minutes, then dry in the sunshine before using.

Tallow Candles

Tallow is the rendered fat of animals, and almost any kind of tallow may be used for candles. Beef tallow makes the hardest and slowest burning. It is an attractive, creamy-white color with a nice luster and a clean odor.

Beef fat also is the cheapest and easiest fat to obtain. It often is available free at your local butcher shop or rendering plant. Just ask if you can have the beef scraps and be willing to pick them up at their convenience.

Render the scraps into tallow by cutting them into small pieces and melting them in a large, heavy pan on the kitchen stove or outdoors over an open fire. Keep the heat down low and be patient. If you have a large pan full it may take several hours. Stir once in a while. When the bits of fried fat float to the top of the melted tallow, strain the hot fat through a piece of cloth and you're ready to make candles.

To Purify Tallow

Tallow used for candles must be clear-grained, perfectly clean fat. It may be purified by boiling 10 minutes in water,

then cooled until the fat solidifies on the surface. Lift the clean tallow off the cold water and dry it with a cloth.
OR

Tallow, beeswax and other ingredients may be melted together with a weak potash or soda lye solution. Let the mixture boil two to three hours, stirring occasionally and straining off impurities that rise to the surface. Chill overnight and lift off the hardened fat.
OR

Dissolve ½ pound alum and ½ pound saltpeter in 1 pint of boiling water. Add 12 ounces beef tallow and simmer over low heat, skimming, for ½ hour. Add 1 cup milk and continue to simmer 15 minutes more. Skim and use for dipping.

Mutton Tallow Candles

Candles may be made from mutton tallow by mixing 3 parts mutton tallow to 1 part beef tallow. Since these candles are likely to be soft and often turn yellow, the following method of hardening may be used:

Melt the tallow over low heat. When nearly melted, stir in 1 pound alum dissolved in a little hot water for each 5 pounds tallow. Stir until melted.
OR

Melt together 1¼ pounds mutton tallow, 8 ounces beeswax, ½ ounce camphor and 4 ounces alum.

Candles from Lard

To 10 pounds melted lard add 1 pound alum dissolved in 1 cup boiling water. Boil until all the water is evaporated, then remove at once from the heat. Skim. Use for molded or dipped candles.

Stearin Candles

Stearin is the principal fatty acid contained in animal fats. Tallow and other fats also contain glycerin and various impurities. To remove these you'll need 3 ounces slaked lime and 4 ounces sulfuric acid for each 1¼ pounds of tallow.

Melt the tallow in a glass or porcelain-lined container and stir in the lime, boiling over low heat until a thick substance is formed. This is lime soap. Add sulfuric acid and stir until the fat separates. The sulfuric acid will unite with the alum, forming sulfate of lime and water. Cool.

CAUTION! Sulfuric acid is **EXTREMELY** caustic. Dispose of the waste in a safe place outdoors.

When cooled remove the solid cake of fat and melt over very low heat, stirring to prevent burning, until any remaining water is boiled off.

You now have stearin, a dry, flammable substance with a pearly luster and no greasy feel. Stearin alone does not make a good candle, but is mixed 1 part wax to 9 parts stearin.

Mixed-Wax Candles

Since wax is the most expensive material for candles, an imitation wax candle can be made by melting together two parts wax to one part tallow. This can be used for dipping or molding. These candles look like wax, but the material is much easier to work with.

To Roll Candles

To roll candles suspend the wicks on a wire frame as for dipping, then hold over the container of melted wax. Pour the wax over the wicks, and what does not adhere will fall back into the container. Continue the process until the candles are the desired size. Roll them one by one to the proper shape with the hands, or you may use wooden paddles which have been soaked in water.

OR

Lay the wicks about 6 inches apart on a cookie sheet covered with wax paper. Pull them straight. Over them pour wax which is warmed enough to pour but not hot. In a few seconds it will be solid enough to cut and roll into a candle shape. Keep the cookie sheet in a warm oven while you work with each candle.

To Mold Candles

Candle molds are available at almost any variety store or hobby shop but they also are available — free of charge — almost everywhere you look. Milk cartons, paper towel rolls, empty plastic bottles, paper cups and cracked tumblers can be found on any trash pile or city dump. All make great, disposable candle molds.

You can use nondisposable molds if

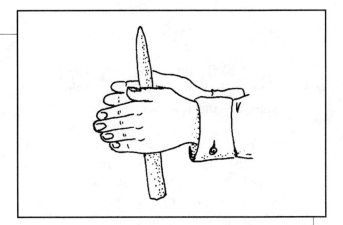

you first make them stick-proof. There are candle sprays and silicone sprays on the market, or you also can use a skillet spray which is made of fat. Or you can dust the inside of the greased mold with talcum powder or kitchen flour.

Candles are molded upside-down, with the upper part of the mold corresponding to the bottom of the candle and the lower part of the mold becoming the candle top. Therefore, the bottom of the mold must have a small piece of excess wick. Preferably it will extend out of the mold, but this may not always be possible. If not, the extra, coiled wick can be pulled out of the candle later.

With molds such as paper cups loop one end of the wick over a wire suspended across the top of the mold, then thread the other end into a large darning needle and push the needle through the bottom of the mold, through the middle of the cup.

OR

The wick may be knotted where it comes out the lower end of the mold to keep it taut. Melted tallow, only hot enough to be easily poured, is poured into the mold until it is filled. Pull the wicks tight and allow the candles to cool. When cold, the candles will have shrunk in the molds. Refill with warm tallow and cool again.

To Dip Candles

First cut the wicks to the proper length, then dip them in melted tallow. After the first dipping, roll the wicks between the fingers to thoroughly incorporate the tallow in the wick, then pull the wick straight and allow it to harden.

When hardened the wicks may be attached to a dipping frame (which allows you to dip several candles at once), made of coat hanger wire. Tie the wicks about three inches apart on the frame and make sure all the wicks will fit into the container of tallow.

Melt the tallow over low heat. The best arrangement is to use two pots, one with an inch or two of boiling water, the other inserted inside it, double-boiler fashion. Be sure the container and the tallow are deep enough for the length of candle you want.

Dip the wicks quickly in the melted tallow. You want to add a layer of tallow each time and yet not melt off the previous layers. It works best if the candle is cold, and some people refrigerate or even freeze them between dippings.

When candles are cold and set, immerse again. Continue until candles are of large enough diameter.

Wrap or box your special candles prettily, with their holders or without, and they will rank high among the nicest gifts you can give.

Except as noted, material in this chapter has been excerpted and adapted from Making Soaps and Candles *of Storey/Garden Way Publishing's Country Kitchen Library.*

CHAPTER 8

Gifts of Flowers

Making Potpourri

Fragrance has the power to arouse forgotten emotions and events. It is memory incarnate, a driving force. It activates the brain in a unique way. It can stimulate and exhilarate, or it can dull the senses. Animals respond to it much as humans do. A sleeping cat is very much awake when a bag of catnip is opened; the dog snoozing on porch steps is suddenly alert when the scent of cat is in the air. The nose remembers even when the body rests.

In the years spent working with fragrance I have seen this memory function at work many times. Weary travelers stopping to visit the herb gardens would suddenly look years younger when a certain aromatic plant took them back to their childhood. Customers in the shop would beg for more of a certain potpourri when some element in the fragrance

recalled a long-forgotten happy memory.

One dictionary defines potpourri as a combination of various incongruous elements. The second definition says it is a mixture of dried flower petals and spices kept in a jar to scent the air. The phrase *pot pourri* comes from the French. The literal translation is "rotten pot." One method of making potpourri from fresh rose petals does result in a rotting process of sorts.

The art of blending potpourri incorporates these two definitions. Some of the recipe ingredients may appear incongruous; combine them all and they play their part in creating fragrance. Basically you will be using dried petals and spices, mixing them with necessary fixatives and oils to create a lasting and pleasing aroma with which to enhance your surroundings and to make gifts for your friends.

A really fine potpourri is a blend of many

fragrances: roses . . . a walk in the woods . . . spices . . . exotic resins and roots, unknown but hauntingly familiar. A well-aged mixture has one predominant aroma and many subordinate ones. Expensive perfumes are blends of as many as 150 fragrances; one of my best potpourris contains 20. As with soup making, the more you put in, the richer the result.

Learning to capture the scent of roses and lavender, recognizing such exotics as frankincense and myrrh, vetiver and tonka bean, and knowing how to blend them all together is rewarding in the creative sense and can add a fresh dimension to life.

From the practical point of view it will enable you to make extended use of a sentimental bouquet of roses. Convert a gift of flowers into a jar of potpourri to give pleasure for years to come.

If you maintain gardens you have a source of fragrant and colorful materials to be dried and used. An herb garden will yield mint, lemon balm, scented-leaf geraniums, lemon verbena, marjoram, lavender, and rosemary for potpourri. A garden of annual flowers produces bright petals that can be dried to add color if not fragrance to your blends. Thus your flowers bloom forever for you in your jars of potpourri.

Uses of Fragrance

Fragrance has been important to man from the earliest recorded events. From Egypt to India, from Greece to China, trade routes were established as early as 2000 B.C.

The first uses of fragrance were for incense to burn in the temples. Then the aristocracy discovered the pleasure of sweet odors in their homes. Early baths were actually great clouds of scented steam enveloping the body. Following the steam session a servant scraped their skin with a smooth tool, removing dead cells and dirt. This was followed by a cooling bath in water perfumed with lemon and later with roses.

The idea of extracting the sweet scent from roses came from an Indian princess about to marry. To prepare the way for the bride, the canals on which the bridal barge would float had been sprinkled with fresh rose petals, much as we scatter them for today's bride. This lovely princess trailed her hands over the side of the barge and found her fingers delightfully fragrant with a thin film of rose oil on them. Thus began the search for the best method of extracting the fragrance from the rose.

What may well be the first instruction book on the art of making potpourri was printed in London in 1779. Called *The Toilet of Flora,* it contains many recipes for cosmetics, tooth powders, hair restorers, and "sweet bags." These bags were meant to be worn on the body or placed in chairs and bedding to release their pleasant odors. The author used cloves and cinnamon, orris root and benzoin, rose petals and lavender, the same ingredients you will find today in my recipes.

Newer mixtures called potpourri appeared on the scene recently. Many contain wood chips, stiff strawflowers, and seed pods of no merit, and have aromas that are overwhelmingly strong when first opened and then quickly evaporate. Other currently popular potpourris are based on fruit and berry fragrances; eventually we may decide these are best left in the ice-cream parlor or bakery.

Master Chart for Potpourri

Potpourri must have one or more elements from each of the following categories in order to have lasting fragrance.

A — Fragrant leaves and flowers

Roses	Lavender	Rosemary	Bay leaves
Mint	Scented geraniums	Lemon verbena	Costmary
Lemon balm	Marjoram	Thyme	Sweet Woodruff

B — Spices and peels

Allspice	Mace	Coriander	Lemon peel
Anise	Cloves	Cinnamon	Orange peel
Nutmeg	Star anise	Cardamom	Vanilla bean

C — Oils, essential or fragrance

Ambergris	Bergamot	Cinnamon	Clove
Jasmine	Lavender	Lemon	Lime
Musk	Neroli	Sweet orange	Bitter orange
Rose	Rose geranium	Sandalwood	Ylang-ylang

D — Fixatives

Orris root	Calamus	Myrrh
Benzoin	Tonka bean	Oakmoss
Cellulose fiber	Vetiver	Frankincense

E — Petals and leaves for color

Pansies	Tulips	Daffodils	Salvias
Calendulas	Larkspur	Geraniums	Delphinium
Carnations	Amaranth	Asters	Uva-ursi (bearberry)
Rose leaves	Ferns	Nigella	Feverfew

Adapted from *Making Potpourri.*

Blending

Nearly every mixture is a blend of different fragrances, just as a fine perfume is a blend. In perfumery *top notes, middle notes,* and *base notes* are carefully balanced to create the distinctive aroma sought by the perfumer.

In a typical rose potpourri the top note might be lavender, the middle note rose, the base note vetiver. Add a second top note of coriander, a second middle note of cinnamon, a second base note of musk, and you have a new and richer scent.

All scents are classified to fit one of these groups; remember to have some from each when you experiment on your own. Most of the recipes given here have scents from each classification. Let's first look at the categories in the master list.

Category A — Fragrant Leaves and Flowers

Of all the flowers you may dry to use in potpourri, only lavender and roses retain their aroma. All the leaves listed have scent glands not easily destroyed by drying; they keep their fragrance indefinitely.

The best roses for fragrance are the antique varieties. We enjoy gathering many petals from the common rugosa roses, but they cannot compare in aroma with my antique gallica and damask roses.

Lavender blossoms hold their perfume almost forever. They contain more oil for their weight than any other fragrant flower. For potpourri pick the flowering stalks when the florets are half open. A bunch placed in an upright basket will dry naturally while adding beauty to the room. All varieties are fragrant; my preference for potpourri is Lavandula vera.

Herb leaves, unlike most flowers, retain their scent when dried; use them freely. Here are properties of some herbs and flowers you can use in potpourri.

Bay leaf — pleasant sharp smell. Does not crumble, so adds shape to the mix.

Costmary — mint scent. Press or dry the leaves.

Lemon balm — lemon scent. Leaves crumble easily.

Lemon verbena — lemon scent. Leaves do not crumble easily.

Sweet marjoram — sweet fragrance. Good in light floral blends.

Spearmint — mint scent. Adds its own note to any mixture.

Rose geranium — rose scent. Leaves may turn brown unless dried in a cold place.

Rosemary — sharp pungency, good color.

Sweet Woodruff — when dried, gives a vanilla fragrance.

Uva-ursi (Arctostaphylos uva-ursi) — leaves hold their green color and shape and are not expensive.

Category B — Spices and Peels

You may already have in your kitchen cupboard many of the seeds and spices listed in the master chart.

Allspice — a combination cinnamon, nutmeg, and clove scent.

Anise seed — slightly licorice, a pleasant and long-lasting aroma.

Star anise — highly aromatic of anise.

Cinnamon — true Ceylon cinnamon is soft, can be crumbled with the fingers and has a sweet odor.

Cardamom — the outer pod and black seeds inside it have a very special pungency. An expensive spice.

Coriander — the seed has a warm sweet fragrance.

Cloves — sharp, spicy scent. Use cloves whole. Use the Rajah variety and add clove oil to them.

Nutmeg — aromatic. The three-layered pod produces both nutmegs and the more expensive mace.

Vanilla bean — luscious aroma, sweet.

Orange and lemon peel — fruit aroma.

Category C — Oils, essential or fragrance

One or more of these fragrant oils are used in every recipe to enhance and perpetuate the aroma you want to achieve. There are two types used: essential and fragrance. In the world of fragrance, *essential oil* is the essence extracted from a plant. An example is lavender oil, produced by extracting the oil present in the flowers by the steam distillation process. If you pack 600 pounds of fresh lavender flowers into a copper tank, cover it securely, and run steam through it, you can obtain about one pint of pure oil. It will drip out of a pipe in the tank into a collecting jar, while the steam will condense to water and run out of another pipe. The resulting oil is then stabilized and sold as essential oil.

In a recipe calling for strawberry oil, you will be using a *fragrance oil*. This is produced chemically in laboratories. The chemist analyzes the smell of strawberries, knows what chemicals contain those components, and blends them to produce a fragrance very close to strawberry.

Basic fragrances important to many traditional potpourris (such as musk, from musk deer, and ambergris, from whales) were once obtained by killing the animals. These ingredients are now reproduced synthetically. Many chemically produced oils are excellent, but you may find great differences in the quality. There is poor quality oil on the market today, but there are also many sources of very good oils.

Oils are highly concentrated and should be measured exactly as directed. Too much of one can ruin a batch of potpourri. In brown glass bottles, tightly closed, and stored in a dark place, they will keep for years. Only poorly made oils lose fragrance quickly. All essential oils are volatile, and will evaporate when exposed to air for long periods.

Category D — Fixatives

A fixative has one main purpose: to preserve your scents. It has the ability to grab and hold the combination of aromas in the jar. Some fixatives will add fragrance, some are scentless.

Fixatives are all of plant origin.

Calamus or sweet flag — sweet smell.

Oakmoss — a lovely earthy smell.

Vetiver or khus-khus — a sweet scent.

Tonka bean — strong vanilla fragrance. Toxic for cooking.

Frankincense — sharp sweet odor when heated.

Myrrh — less balsamic odor than frankincense. Both are gum resins and have been used for centuries as aromatics, as medications, for embalming, and as incense in the temples.

Benzoin — another gum resin which fuses all the aromatics.

Orris root — a faint violet aroma. An old reliable fixative.

Cellulose fiber (ground corncobs) — low cost, absorbent, nonallergenic, effective.

Although I still use orris root for most of my recipes, many successful potpourris use cellulose and oil to fix fragrance. One teaspoon (⅛ ounce) oil plus 1 cup cellulose fiber will scent and fix about 8 cups of potpourri. In recipes calling for more than one oil, please use separate jars. Measure the cellulose into each jar, add the oil, let each mellow overnight, then add to the botanicals.

Some general rules for fixatives: Using orris root or oakmoss, put botanicals and spices into container and mix well. Put orris root or oakmoss on the surface. Add oils. Stir thoroughly.

When fixing with frankincense, myrrh, benzoin, vetiver, or tonka bean, mix together all ingredients except oils. Add oil then mix again.

When you are using spices and their oils, drop oils onto spices. Mix well.

Category E — Dried petals and leaves

While only roses and lavender flowers retain their scent after drying, most blossoms and leaves are worth drying to add color and dimension to potpourri.

Some mixtures of dried rose buds, lavender, leaves, spices, and fixatives can look quite drab in a glass jar. Add a few bright red tulip petals, deep pink larkspur, or true blue delphinium — and the mixture glows with light. Lemon scented potpourris are a good place for yellow shades. Dry calendulas for this purpose.

Most flowers will dry well if spread in a single layer in shallow boxes placed in a warm, airy location. Direct sunlight is acceptable if the temperature is high enough to dry the petals quickly, say in 24 hours. Prolonged exposure to bright light will fade colors.

Pansies and ferns should be pressed in a thick catalog or paperback book without glossy pages. Place the pansies face down as flat as possible on the page, cover with the next pages. Repeat until all flowers or pages are used, weight the book with any heavy object, and leave it for a week or ten days. You will have a good supply of flat, dry flowers to add their pretty faces to potpourri. Ferns and lacy leaves, dried the same way, retain their good green color.

Floral designers sweep up and discard fallen petals and blooms at the end of the day. Should you know anyone who works in either fresh or dried flower design, you may well have an unfailing source of potpourri flowers.

Putting It All Together

There are hundreds of recipes for potpourri, but only two different ways to make it: the moist or the dry method.

Since it has been recorded that the Egyptians buried clay pots of rose petals in the sand to be exhumed and inhaled at a later date, we could say they were the first to make potpourri by the moist method.

This process is rarely used today, since few of us have access to large quantities of the really fragrant, antique roses. First, gather a peck or so of petals. Spread these out on screens or trays to partially dry; two days is enough. They will shrink in volume by about a third. Next, pack them tightly into any straight-sided glass or pottery container. Layer every three inches of petals with ½ cup of pure, noniodized salt. Place a plate over the surface and weight it down with something heavy to keep the roses compressed. Store in a warm dark place for about three weeks.

Invite your best friends in for the unveiling. When you remove the plate, the absolutely incredible fragrance of roses is too much to keep all to yourself. It is an experience rarely duplicated.

If it is not totally dry, stir it well, compress it again and let it keep curing. The result will be a dry cake of unappetizing color, but heavenly aroma. Now you can add spices, orange peel, and a few aromatic fixatives, and have a potpourri that should hold its aroma for fifty years.

The dry method is the usual way we mix potpourri, both on a small scale at the kitchen table and in large amounts commercially. The hobbyist uses a glass jar, the commercial operation uses a cement mixer. All ingredients must be dry. Simply measure out the botanical ingredients, add the properly prepared spices, then stir in the oils and fixatives.

When using cellulose fiber, add the fixative and age this for a day or two before incorporating it into the other ingredients. For all my recipes using orris root I have consistent good results when I put the botanicals and spices in the jar, stir well, place the orris root on the surface,

then start adding the oils. Most of the oil is absorbed by the orris root; the remainder clings to rosebuds or bits of vetiver or moss. At the last I thoroughly stir and shake, or pour the mixture back and forth several times, until every bit of oil-soaked orris root has said "hello" to every other ingredient.

Always remember that the fragrance you achieve when the mixing is finished is not final. All dry potpourris need at least three weeks to mellow and tone down. Trust your recipe, not your nose, when you smell a freshly made batch. Shake it daily, let it rest in a dark place, and notice the gradual mellowing of the scent. If after three weeks you are still not satisfied with the fragrance, modify it by adding a few drops of whatever you think it needs.

Necessary Tools

Most of the matériel you will need for making potpourris can be found in your own kitchen or purchased inexpensively. Things I consider necessary include:

An old three-speed blender (for cracking whole spices).

Several old measuring cups and set of spoons.

Clean glass jars. One-quart mayonnaise jars are fine for small batches.

Wooden paddles or spoons for stirring.

Dieter's scales for measuring ounces.

Inexpensive glass eyedroppers. Ideally you should use a clean one for each oil.

For larger batches, you will need 5-gallon containers. I use the food grade plastic pails available at bakeries. Lightweight plastic will not do. Glass, stoneware, stainless steel, make the containers preferred by the professionals in this business. Since buying oils at the Fragonard factory in France where they package all oils and perfumes in aluminum, I must add this metal to the suitable container list.

Recipes

All the recipes here will be based on the dry method. They use materials that may be purchased at any time of year.

This basic rose mixture might be the one to try if you have received a bouquet of roses and want their memory to live on. You need to purchase only an ounce of cut orris root and a small vial of rose oil. Coarsely cracked spices are best, but for your first attempt you might use ground spices from the cupboard.

Small Rose Jar

2 cups dried rose petals and leaves
½ teaspoon each of cinnamon, cloves,
    and allspice
1½ teaspoons orris root
6 drops rose oil

Combine the first 4 ingredients in a quart jar. Add orris root and drop the oil onto it. Shake well. Age for 3 weeks, shaking daily. This light rose fragrance keeps well.

Classic Rose Potpourri

This is a rich blend with hints of garden and woods as well as the strong rose scent.

Combine thoroughly in a gallon jar:
1 quart rose petals
1 to 2 cups lavender flowers
1 to 2 cups rose geranium leaves
½ cup patchouli leaves
¼ cup sandalwood chips
¼ cup vetiver root
1 cup rosemary

Mix, then add:
2 teaspoons frankincense
1 teaspoon myrrh
1 teaspoon coarsely ground cloves
1 teaspoon crushed Ceylon cinnamon
2 tonka beans, ground or broken

Mix together, then add:
1 cup orris root
30 drops rose oil

Stir all together thoroughly. Age for 3 weeks.

Spicy Rose Potpourri

This blend is quite inexpensive to make. It holds its fragrance well, looks nice in glass containers, and smells wonderful in sachets. A good recipe to make to sell at a church fair.

In a gallon jar, combine:

1 quart red rose petals

1 quart uva-ursi leaves

2 cups oakmoss

2 cups cellulose and rose oil (mixed as suggested on page 130)

2 cups citrus-spice potpourri (see page 136)

Mix all this. It smells good the same day, even better after aging.

Lavender Potpourri

Lavender is said to have been Queen Victoria's favorite scent. She showed uncommon good sense in most things; what she preferred in fragrance has remained a favorite to this day. Please do not think of lavender fragrance as just something for old ladies and bed linens. Aroma therapists tell us that inhaling lavender fragrance is calming to the spirit; it appears to have that effect on all of us.

The following blend is very nice to use in sachet bags. Use light blue petals such as delphinium or bachelor button for added color if displaying it in glass jars.

Lavender Bouquet

4 cups lavender flowers

1 cup oakmoss

4 teaspoons cracked cloves

2 teaspoons cracked allspice

½ cup crushed Ceylon cinnamon

1 vanilla bean

½ cup orris root

1 teaspoon each oils of lavender and bergamot

Combine the first 5 ingredients in a gallon jar. Cut the vanilla bean into small pieces and add. Stir it all well. Scatter the orris root on surface and add the oils. Now stir very well, cover and let age.

Apple Spice Potpourri

For this recipe, first prepare some apple slices. Sprinkle about 1 teaspoon of grated nutmeg onto a metal pie pan. Cut 1 large apple into quarters, remove core, slice into thin pieces. Now lay these pieces on the pie pan, sprinkle with more nutmeg and dry until leathery. The mantel over our wood stove is perfect during fall and winter for this sort of drying. Any source of low, dry heat will do: the top of a radiator, a gas or electric oven preheated to 150° F., then the heat turned off. In about two days the slices will be dry and you can proceed.

Put 1 cup of 1-inch cinnamon stick in a quart jar, drop 7 drops of cinnamon oil on it. Allow to rest for a day. Then put ½ cup red rosehips in the jar, treat them to 12 drops apple-spice oil and shake well. Now add the apple slices dried with nutmeg and shake the whole thing together. This potpourri smells heavenly as soon as it is blended and it improves even more with aging.

Maine Blueberry Potpourri

Another popular fragrance here in Maine is Blueberry potpourri. I do not make it, but if I did I would use this recipe.

3 cups white amaranth flowers

3 cups uva-ursi

3 cups juniper berries

2 cups purple malva blossoms

1 cup cellulose fiber with 1 teaspoon
    blueberry oil

Freshening Potpourri

To put fresh vitality into a tired potpourri simply pour it back into a glass jar, add bits of fresh spices, another pinch of orris root and several drops of the predominant oil fragrance. Shake it up and then replace in the open container. It will be good for several more months.

Treat the blueberry fragrance oil to an overnight visit with the cellulose fiber, then combine all ingredients in a gallon jar and mix well. Aging will improve the already delicious blueberry scent.

The best oil for this one is sometimes found in shops selling scented oils for candle making.

Potpourris from the Woods

There are many variations for a woodsy theme. If you have access to fir balsam tips, beechnut burrs, cedar tips and cones, mosses, dried rose hips, and juniper berries, you can make large amounts of low-cost potpourris and scented pillows.

The simplest way to make your own fir balsam pillow is to clip new light green June growth from fully grown fir balsam trees, dry tips and pack them tightly into a square of fabric you have sewn together.

It is important to identify the tree before gathering any needles. Put your thumb and forefinger on the top and bottom of a branch. If all the needles are lying flat, and do not prick your fingers, you have fir balsam. The needles are soft by comparison with the prickly and unsuitable spruce.

Fir balsam provides the Christmas trees and wreaths preferred by many. This basic recipe has a clean forest scent.

Maine Woods Air

1 cup fir balsam tips
½ cup rose hips
½ cup juniper berries
½ cup hemlock cones
¼ cup oakmoss

Combine everything in a jar with the oakmoss on top. Sprinkle 10 drops fir balsam oil onto it. Stir well, shake and age.

Holiday Potpourri: Create a bright mixture similar to the above, adding red sumac berries, some red geranium and rose petals, and Christmas fragrance oil.

From the East Coast . . .

Bayberry Potpourri

Most of us know the warm, balsamic aroma of bayberry candles since every gift shop seems to sell them. My version of bayberry potpourri came into being many years ago when we were vacationing along the coast and noticing the wonderful fragrance from the leaves of this shrub.

With a little imagination, you can make a potpourri with almost the same aroma.

1 cup uva-ursi leaves
½ cup oakmoss
½ cup juniper berries
½ cup cellulose fiber and ½ teaspoon
    bayberry oil

Mix the cellulose and oil and allow to set for 24 hours. Then add the other ingredients. Shake and age. You may adjust the scent with more leaves or more oil. Try packaging this one in a large empty clam shell.

. . . To the Far East

The heavy aromas of patchouli, sandalwood, and musk are definitely exotic. They speak of temples and incense, of Hindu ladies in saris, Tibetan monks at prayer. These scents are very pleasing in potpourri and combine well with vetiver and roses, spices and citrus peel.

This recipe never fails to please.

Bombay Nights

4 tablespoons sandalwood chips
½ cup patchouli leaves
2 cups lavender flowers
2 teaspoons chopped tonka bean
½ cup dried orange peel
1 tablespoon crushed Ceylon cinnamon
½ cup cut vetiver root
5 cardamom pods, broken
1 teaspoon frankincense
1 teaspoon myrrh
10 drops patchouli oil
5 drops sandalwood oil

Combine everything except the oils in a quart jar. Drop the oils on the surface and stir in. Shake thoroughly and age. A few drops of bitter orange oil are nice in this one.

Make Your Own Simmering Scents

In the early 1970s when oil prices rose steeply overnight, woodstoves came back into vogue for most of us living in the cold belt of the country. Soon every purveyor of potpourri was packaging and marketing "simmering scents." These were fragrant mixtures to be added to water and simmered on the stove top. They accomplished two things: the steam added moisture to the warm dry air generated by the woodstove, and it carried good smells throughout the house.

Citrus-Spice Potpourri

We mix this one in the largest container we have. Sometimes a batch is started with five pounds of star anise and cinnamon, so you can see we end up with a lot of good smells. Here is a mini-version to get you started.

1 cup 1-inch cinnamon sticks
1 cup whole allspice
2 cups star anise
1 cup coriander
2 cups dried orange peel
½ cup cloves
½ cup crushed nutmegs
10 drops cinnamon oil
10 drops allspice oil
20 drops sweet orange oil

Use a gallon jar for this one. As you put each spice into it, add the corresponding oil directly onto it and shake well. When everything is in, shake and stir thoroughly. Let age at least 1 day for the spices to absorb the oils before using. Like all potpourris, the longer it ages the richer it smells.

This is the recipe used in Spicy Rose potpourri. It is a mixture that allows for endless variation. Ginger root, mace, vanilla bean, cardamom and tonka bean could be added. Use plenty of citrus peel. Lemon and tangerine peel would be nice here.

Some New Potpourri Recipes

All the recipes given so far are those I adapted from books in print for many years. There were no other resources available when I began making good scents from the plants in my herb gardens.

At a perfume workshop I finally learned the formula for blending pleasing fragrances. I have mentioned the necessary top, middle and base notes. All scents are in one of these categories; proper proportions bring them into balance.

This new knowledge led me to analyze my old, trusted recipes. Sure enough, the best ones had the right balance. With my lists of top, middle, and base note fragrances in hand, I developed new recipes. I am sharing some of them with you, with the category indicated for elements of scent.

Melody

(T) ½ cup coriander
(T) ½ cup lavender
(M) 1 cup rose petals
¼ cup oakmoss
½ cup vetiver
1 teaspoon benzoin granules
(T) 5 drops bois de rose oil
(T) 3 drops bay oil
(M) 5 drops rose oil
(M) 5 drops neroli oil
(B) 3 drops sandalwood oil
(B) 4 drops patchouli oil
(M) ¼ teaspoon heliotropin crystals

Mix coriander, rose petals, lavender, vetiver and benzoin together. Add oakmoss and onto it place the oils. Stir very well; age at least a month. This one just gets better.

Jasmine Potpourri

(M) 1 cup pink rose petals
1 cup purple petals, any kind
(M) 1 tablespoon crushed Ceylon cinnamon
1 teaspoon benzoin granules
¼ cup oakmoss
(B) 12 drops pure jasmine oil
(B) 5 drops patchouli oil
(T) 4 drops bois de rose
(T) 3 drops lavender oil

Add oakmoss last to the dry materials, drop on the oils. Age at least a month.

Springsong Potpourri

(M) 1 cup rosebuds
1 cup uva-ursi
¼ cup vetiver
1 teaspoon benzoin granules
(M) 1 tablespoon crushed Ceylon cinnamon
½ cup oakmoss
(M) 6 drops ylang-ylang oil
(T) 5 drops lime oil
(B) 3 drops patchouli oil
(M) 3 drops jasmine oil

Blend; add oakmoss last. Drop on the oils. Shake well and age. It becomes a heavenly, light floral scent after one month.

Drying and Preserving Flowers for Bouquets

In addition to the flowers that can be picked and used right away in delightful arrangements, there are many flowers that are better for arranging when dried or preserved. Many garden flowers and wildflowers may be dried by using a desiccant or by hanging them upside down to air dry, but some flowers tolerate it better than others.*

To learn more about growing trees, flowers, and shrubs for arranging, see The Flower Arranger's Garden, *Country Wisdom Bulletin A-103.*

Drying Agents

Desiccant comes in three forms: borax, sand, or a silica gel, all of which absorb moisture from the flower. Differ-ent mixtures to try are: borax; half borax and half corn meal; half borax and half white silica builder's sand; fine white builder's sand; and Flower Dri and similar products. Many different flowers may be dried using this method. Its benefit is that the flower's color is preserved well. Its disadvantage is that it is rather time consuming, and the boxes filled with the drying agent can take up quite a bit of room. Desiccants are probably the best way to preserve those special blooms of roses, daffodils, and zinnias. Any garden flower may be tried.

The process is simple enough. Cut the flowers on a sunny day before they have reached full maturity and when the colors are clear and true. Strip the leaves from the stalks and place stalks lengthwise in desiccant. Place round flowers such as zinnias, chrysanthemums, marigolds and anemones face down. Cover the flowers gently with more of the mixture.

Sachets for Mothproofing

Several herbs which can be purchased from the supply sources listed or easily grown in your garden have proven to repel moths. If you have always relied on mothballs or flakes to keep your woolens intact, you may like the more pleasant smell to be had from botanicals.

Wormwood, southernwood, and tansy are the herbs grown here in quantity to supply my demand for "herbal mothballs." Other herbs include santolina, pennyroyal, and mint. In late summer cut the long stems and bunch with elastics, then hang in the warm attic to dry. Later strip and combine them in a five-gallon pail ready for use.

Each herb has its own strong and pungent scent. To temper the somewhat acrid odor I add handfuls of cedar shavings and lavender flowers to each pail (they in themselves are also moth repellents.)

Just two or three botanicals are enough to make herbal moth balls. You do not need fixatives or oils. To hold the mixture, cut 6-inch squares of any firm fabric. Put about one-quarter cup of blend in center of square. With your fingers gather up the fabric to make a ball; tie tightly with a long length of yarn. Make a double bow with loops big enough to slip over a coat hanger. Half a dozen are enough for a good-sized closet. One or two will take care of a drawer. These remain effective so long as the scent is there, at least two years.

Plants and Flowers for Hanging

Achillea — These flowers will dry on the plant, but may be hung to dry.

Artemisia

Globe amaranth

Baby's breath

Bells of Ireland

Delphinium

Fern fronds

Globe thistle (*Echinops* **species)** — the mature flowers dry well when hung or placed in a glycerine solution.

Lavender

Sage

Sea lavender (*Limonium* **species)** — Cut the stems when the flowers are mature and hang in a warm room for two to four weeks. Its colors preserve well.

Strawflower (*Helichrysum* **species)** is excellent when dried for winter. The flowers will dry naturally on the plant but you may want to pick them before they fully mature. Pick the flower heads and immediately mount them on florist's wire. Insert the wire in the top of the flower and hook it behind the petals. Then either hang them upside down or push them into a block of Oasis to dry, which usually takes three to four weeks.

Some Wildflowers that Dry Well
Without Using a Desiccant

Bergamot	Goldenrod	Pussy willow
Black-eyed susan	Joe-Pye weed	Tansy
Butterfly weed	Milkweed	Teasel
Cattail	Mullein	
Dock	Pearly everlasting	

Plants with attractive seed pods for dried arrangements:

Bittersweet	Globe thistle	Lily
Chinese lantern	Honesty	Poppy
Columbine	Iris	Conifers
Delphinium		

The traditional way to dry flowers is to cut them on a dry, sunny day, strip the foliage from the stems, group the stems in small bunches and tie together with a rubber band, and hang them upside down. Choose a spot for drying which is warm, dry, and has good air circulation. Hang large or thick stems, such as those of delphinium, separately. The length of drying time depends on the structure of the plant. Plants with thin stems and a thin, papery texture will dry faster than those with thick stems and dense texture. Check the plants often as they dry.

Xeranthemum dries very well. The small flowers come in light pink shades. Dry them away from bright light to keep their color.

Glycerine as Foliage Preservative

Glycerine is an excellent material used to preserve foliage for arranging. Place the stems in a glass jar to a depth of three inches in a solution of glycerine (⅓ glycerine to ⅔ water). Keep the jar in a cool room and check the foliage every day. When it is pliable, remove the stems and lay them in a box to dry. You can store the dried branches in a box lined with newspaper, or keep them upright in a container. Beech leaves, Elaeagnus, holly, magnolia, and oak preserve well in glycerine.

Grasses

Arranging with dried materials doesn't have to be limited to flowers. Many grasses add a distinctive touch to an arrangement. Some to include are zebra grass and maiden grass (*Miscanthus* species), purple moor grass (*Molinia caerulea*), and *Pennisetum* species. Many wild grasses can be cut for use in arrangements.

The tall heads of grass seed blend well with preserved material. Fresh grasses need almost no conditioning. To use them dry, leave them in the garden to dry naturally before cutting. Or, before they are fully mature, cut them (with long stems) and hang to dry in a cool, dark place.

Cutting and Conditioning Fresh Flowers

Success in flower arranging depends on knowing the best ways to condition and maintain plant materials to keep them looking fresh. Conditioning is the plant's process of taking on more water than it gives off, so as to put it into a prime state of freshness. It is all-important for creating flower arrangements that will last for more than a day.

The rules for conditioning most flowers are the same but there are specific things to do for various blooms. One rule is certain: it is best to cut plant material in the evening, because sugar has been stored in the plant tissue all day. The next best time to cut is early morning, and the poorest time is midday. You have to plan ahead.

Cut flowers with a sharp knife or garden clippers. Cut the stem on a slant and remove all unnecessary foliage. As soon as the flower is cut, place the stem up to its neck in warm water and place the flowers in a cool room for at least six hours or overnight. A darkened room will slow the development of the blooms. Any that you want to open should be placed close to an indirect light source.

Some stems need special treatment. Brittle stems (such as on chrysanthe-mums) should be broken to expose a greater surface for water intake. Woody stems (lilac) should be peeled back and split an inch or so. Milky stems (poppies) must be sealed with flame, or by dipping the end quickly in boiling water. Milky stems need to be resealed each time they are cut, so they are not suitable for needle-point holders, which pierce the stem.

Cut foliage plants when they are mature. Remove tender new growth. Most foliage can be immersed completely and some must be. Wilted plant material is not necessarily dead; it may be just thirsty. Recut the stems and place in hot water and most will revive. After conditioning, place the plant material in cool water in a cool room.

Some commercial chemical prepara-tions added to the water in which plants are conditioned have value in that they check maturing, nourish plants, sweeten the water and help slow decay. Other tips are: remove the pollen from self-pollinat-ing flowers; cut stems under water to keep air bubbles from entering (important with roses); put water in the container before you start the arrangement; and cut the stems straight across for needlepoint holders, and on an angle for deep vases.

Arranging

Flower arrangers need more than a vase. There are many devices that make the task of holding flowers where you want them a whole lot easier.

Certain items are essential to the art of arranging; others are just handy. All you really need to get started are some con-tainers in the basic shapes, assorted needlepoint holders (also called pin holders) and other stem-securing equipment, a sharp knife or flower shears, and florist's tape or clay. The following list gives you an idea of what you may like to have. Items preceded by an asterisk are essential.

Pin holders come in a variety of sizes and shapes and will last forever.

Oasis is used with or without a pin holder to hold the material in an arrangement in place. It can be purchased at your local florist or garden center, comes in block form and may be cut to size with a sharp knife.

Florist's clay is used to secure the holder to the container.

Styrofoam is used for arranging dried material.

Clippers and a *sharp knife* are essential.

Florist's wire is used to wire stems so they will bend.

Florist's tape is used to cover the wire.

Bleach, 1 teaspoon to a quart of water, will keep the water clean and lengthen the life of the arrangement.

Pebbles in different colors and sizes can be used to cover holders.

A *lazy susan* is handy to have for turning the arrangement while you work on it.

Stands and *bases* can be used with the container to improve the design.

The Flower Arrangement

There are many types of flower arrangement, ranging from formal styles with strict rules of form and design, to the casual mix of flowers in a basket.

Many books tell how to arrange flowers, so we'll just go over the basics here and let the gardener/arranger go by feel for the rest. There are almost no rules that have to be observed, but if you understand some principles of good design it will help give you confidence in what you are doing.

Principles of Design

Proportion. Your flower arrangement is in good proportion when it appears to be the right size for its container. In a tall vase, a rule of thumb is to have the height of the arrangement equal to 1½ to 2 times the height of the vase. This rule also holds for wide, horizontal containers, in which the tallest stem should be 1½ to 2 times the width or diameter of the bowl. This rule, of course, may be broken, but following it when beginning to make flower arrangements can simplify the task.

Balance. Arrangements are said to be balanced when they give a sense of stability, and do not appear lopsided. Symmetrical balance is achieved when both halves of the arrangement are identical or nearly identical. In asymmetry the two halves are not the same, yet they appear to be balanced, or to have equal importance.

Texture. It is a good idea to include contrasting textures in an arrangement: use glossy foliage with soft flowers, or sleek leaves with rough, ruffled blossoms. Nature gives us many choices here.

Color. So much can be said about color. Sometimes a flower arrangement can be enhanced by using hues of greater and lesser value in the same color family. Dark colors work well in the base of an

Conditioning Flowers for Fresh Bouquets

Flower	When to Cut	Treatment for Conditioning
Anemone	½ to fully open	Scrape stems
Aster	¾ to fully open	Scrape stems
Azalea	Bud to fully open	Scrape and crush stems
Bachelor's button	½ to fully open	Scrape and crush stems
Bleeding heart	4 or 5 florets open	Scrape stems
Calendula	Fully open	Scrape stems
Carnation	Fully open; snap or break from plant	Scrape stems
Chrysanthemum	Fully open; break off	Scrape or crush stems
Daffodil	As color shows in bud	Cut foliage sparingly and scrape stems
Dahlia	Fully open	Sear stems in flame
Daisy	½ to fully open	Scrape stems or sear in flame
Delphinium	¾ to fully open	Scrape stems, break off top buds
Gladiolus	As second floret opens	Scrape stems
Iris	As first bud opens	Leave foliage, scrape stems
Lilac	½ to fully open	Scrape and crush stems; put wilted branches in very hot water for 1 hour
Lily	As first bud opens	Cut no more than ⅓ of stem
Marigold	Fully open	Scrape stems
Peony	Bud in color or fully open	Scrape or split stems
Poppy	Night before opening	Sear stems; a drop of wax in heart of flower keeps it open
Rose	As second petal unfurls; cut stem just above a five-petal leaf	Scrape stems; cut stems again while holding under water
Tulip	Bud to ½ open	Cut foliage sparingly, scrape stems, stand in deep water overnight
Zinnia	Fully open	Sear stems in flame

arrangement, as they look heavier. Colors are usually related to what's in a room — contrasting or blending in with — and white can work in just about any room.

Form. Flowers and leaves come in many different shapes and sizes (for example, rounded tulips with their spear-shaped leaves), and it is a good idea to make use of these different forms when making a flower arrangement. Often, as is the case with a tulip, the flower's own foliage is contrast enough. But mixing different foliage and flowers is the usual practice to obtain the contrast you are looking for.

Basic Shapes for Arrangements

Beginning an arrangement with a finished design in mind can often be easier than if you have no idea of what the finished product will look like. Many arrangements have basic geometric shapes. If you keep a shape in mind while arranging the flowers your arrangement will come together more quickly.

Many factors help determine what shape to use. Some of these include: the kind of flowers and foliage you are using, where the arrangement will go in the home (a tall arrangement would not work in the center of the dining table), and the size and shape of the container you are using.

Shapes to consider:

Circular. This popular shape is satisfying to use and admire. Many round flowers, such as asters and zinnias, work well in this kind of arrangement. One way to avoid a too-round look is to use contrasting foliage with the round flowers.

Triangular. This is a basic shape for many symmetrical arrangements. It can be used with many variations of height and width and works well with low and wide or tall and narrow containers. The first step is to establish lines of height and width, usually with taller branches of a long-stemmed flower or foliage. Select ones that are paler in color or more delicate in form. Then make a focal point with a large bloom or a group of flowers at the center and just above the rim of the container. Fill in with flowers of different lengths, grouping colors together rather

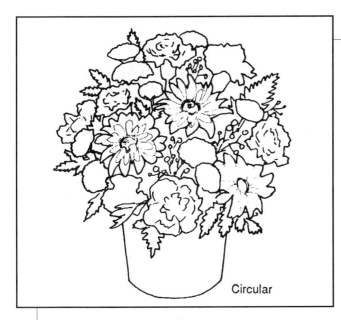

Circular

Styles of Arrangements

There are many styles of flower arrangements and these are good to know about, through you would probably use a specific style only if you were entering a flower show.

Traditional arrangements include both Occidental and Oriental. Occidental includes all the European "period" styles, including Early American and Colonial Williamsburg. These are mostly mass arrangements, as seen in the paintings by the old Dutch masters. Oriental arrangements are an art in themselves and often strive for simplicity. Japanese arrangements are usually made around three main lines with some auxiliary lines, cut to very

than placing them randomly in the arrangement.

Crescent. The crescent is an asymmetrical arrangement that is more difficult to achieve. You need to use flowers with stems that can be bent so you can achieve the curve you are looking for.

Line. Line arrangements can also be difficult to do but are worth the extra effort. In modern line arrangements, a branch can be the focal point and the flowers become secondary. A vertical line is useful when you don't have much space for an arrangement. Tall, spiked flowers such as the gladiolus with its own foliage can work well here. Another line arrangement, used a great deal in flower shows, is the Hogarth curve, a rhythmic line in the shape of a long 's' curve. You can achieve it by first using pliable branches to make the curve and then filling in with flowers.

Convex curve. This curve is a good one to use when you make a centerpiece for a table, as it does not have to be tall. The arrangement is symmetrical and should look attractive when viewed from all sides.

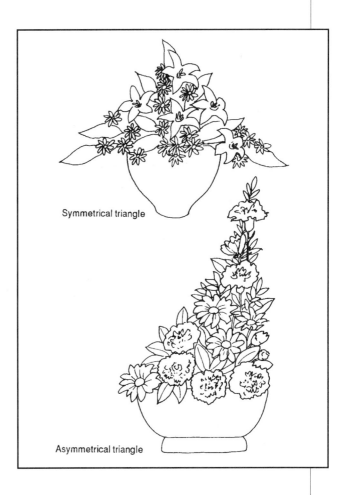

Symmetrical triangle

Asymmetrical triangle

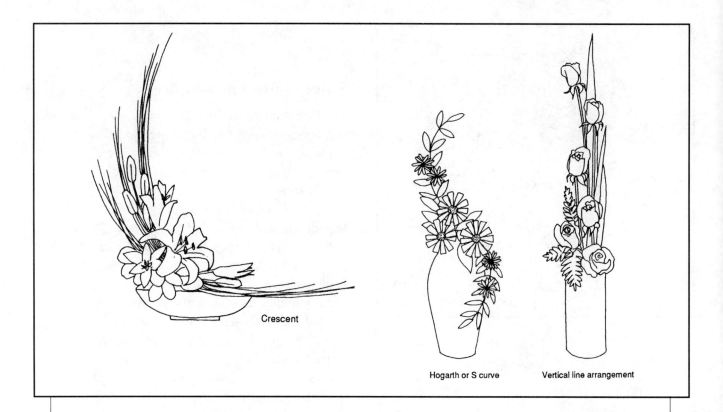

Crescent

Hogarth or S curve

Vertical line arrangement

specific proportions. Studying these can help when creating arrangements for the home and for gifts.

Conventional arrangements are based on geometric form, or line. In some designs, the line is the dominant feature while in others it is used to create shapes such as curves. Additional plant material is brought into many arrangements to strengthen the basic shape. Whereas a true line arrangement may be only one lovely branch and flower, a mass-line or mass arrangement will have many flowers and leaves filling in the basic shape.

Perhaps a miniature arrangement, no bigger than three inches in any direction, is called for. These are fun to try and can be more of a challenge than a large mass arrangement.

In whatever form — a fresh bouquet, a lovely dried arrangement, or a grandly scented jar of potpourri — you know that gifts of flowers are always welcome.

Except as noted, material in this chapter has been excerpted and adapted from Making Potpourri *(A-130) and* The Flower Arranger's Garden *(A-103), both Storey/ Garden Way Publishing Country Wisdom Bulletins.*

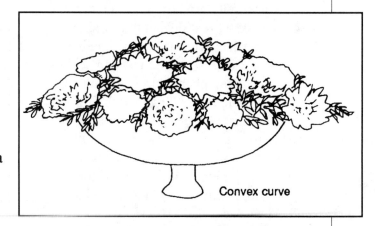

Convex curve

CHAPTER 9

Packaging Your Gifts

Now that you've created several of the items in this book, how can you attractively present these fine homemade gifts?

First, take no chances of spoilage. Keep fresh things fresh. Condition fresh flowers before arranging. Seal and process jellies, jams, pickles, and sauces as recipes direct. Cork or cap wines, liqueurs, and vinegars. Exclude air from baked goods and candies. Refrigerate or freeze food items where necessary.

But: allow soaps to cure (to age out their early caustic properties) before giving them as gifts. *Label* things. A terrific flavored vinegar might look a lot like wine. A simmering potpourri, no matter how enticing it smells, is not for making tea. In a note (or on the label) tell the recipient.

Sanitize containers if you're putting foods in them. Make sure all items of packaging — especially reused ones — are clean. Test to see that gift items will come *out* once they are *in*. On the other hand, devise secure, sturdy containers for carrying pies, cakes, glassed goods of all kinds, and flowers.

A fine touch in presenting homemade gifts is to include recipes for their use. (With, say, jam, a small loaf of your perfect bread would make its own statement.) Best of all, of course, include a copy of *Country Fresh Gifts*.

Packaging Materials

Think out the packaging ahead of time. Cover or paint containers, and color-spray or glitter-spray bows or decorations early enough so they will be dry and free of paint scent before placing them near food.

Containers. Right away, we think of boxes and cartons and sacks. Remember too that any reusable container can become part of the gift. Consider:

Baskets

Tin cans, spray-painted or glittered, or covered with Con-Tact paper. Plastic lids will fit these.

Clear plastic fast-food containers with lids

Bowls

Cups

Saucers, plates, or platters

Trays

Bottles and jugs

Jars or glasses — all sizes, all varieties

Reusable loaf pans

Disposable cake or pie pans

Wrapping Papers. Some surprising things can be used for wrapping presents.

Gift Wrap: occasions, holidays, birthdays

Construction paper

Purchased gift bags

Wallpaper samples

White or colored typing paper

Plain paper sacks, decorated with stenciled or potato-printed designs, or with fabric-paint scenes; or trimmed with gold or silver spray or colored glitter, or even strips of outrageously fake fur

Foils — gold, silver, or colored

Ribbon. Try something a little different.

New ropelike neon hair cords

Stretchy colored gift cord

Satin gift ribbon, one or more colors

Printed gift ribbon

Cloth ribbon which can become a hair ribbon

New long colored shoestrings. Use a pair, or two!

Bungee cord (the heavy elastic cable with a J-hook on each end provides another gift)

Binder twine or twisted paper package twine. Leave ends long. Separately make a multilooped bow, and gild or glitter-spray it. When it's dry and paint scent is gone, fasten to package.

Packaging Ideas

Sample Pack. Fill a gift set of mugs with wrapped candies, a potpourri sachet, small soaps, a jar of relish or special sauce, stick pretzels, and a candle or two. Place in decorated box and leave the lid off.

Bread. Line a clean rectangular basket with a new kitchen towel. In the basket place a loaf of home-baked bread, sealed first in plastic or waxed paper. Fold the towel over the bread. Tie a colorful ribbon both ways over basket and all. Put a bow on top. Carry by the basket, not the ribbon.

Multi-Gift. An open box with a fluffy effect. Cover a carton inside and outside with plain gift paper. Wrap separately small jars of jellies or pickles, some cookies, a candle, and flavored vinegar. Place in box. Wedge varicolored tissue in around the jars, leaving points of papers sticking up.

Jams or Pickles. Package in a new dishcloth or kitchen towel. Place jar in center, bring up shorter sides and tape in place. Bring up long sides and arrange them. Tie a ribbon (once) or a fancy elastic cord (twice) around the neck.

Floral Arrangement. Make a miniature arrangement in a teacup. Fasten it inside the cup with floral clay. Pile a matching saucer with your special candies.

Using clear plastic wrap, place the cup in the center of a sheet large enough to form a tented top. Bring up the plastic wrap loosely and fasten with colored tape and a bow. Make a similar package for the saucer. Place packages on a tray.

Cookies. Arrange pyramid style on a gift platter. Or place in rows on edge in a fast-food container. For a large quantity, use a foil-lined shoebox. Make a tented package, or put in a gift sack. Decorate with ribbon and a bow.

Cake. Bake it in a new pan; present it, iced and decorated, in the pan. Or place it on a gift plate or tray. Or buy cardboard base shapes and boxes at a bakery or pizzeria. Decorate box *before* you put cake in.

Bottled Gifts. Fill a small basket or wire container with straw packing and various small bottles to create a sampler pack.

- Fill a nice decanter with wine or liqueur and give with decorative glasses.

- Give a pound of coffee beans with your liqueur to a coffee-lover friend.

Bottling Ideas for Wines, Liqueurs, and Vinegars

Save attractive bottles. Soak off labels. Sanitize and reuse liquor, beer, or soda bottles; 16-ounce Grolsch beer bottles have an attached reclosable ceramic cap, making them ideal. Look for unique shaped bottles at flea markets, rummage and garage sales, and the town dump; they will make your bottled gifts look and even taste that much better! Check kitchen or import stores for small cupsize bottles and create six-pack samplers.

Bottle corks of all sizes may be pur-chased at winemaking shops for capping bottles. Soda bottle caps come in a variety of styles and colors. Cover the cork or cap with foil, tie a ribbon across the top, and seal with a wax sealer. Check commercial bottles for other techniques.

For wrapping the bottles, the simplest way is tissue paper in various colors, tied around the neck of the bottle with a satin ribbon. You can also use the brightly colored bags sold by many gift shops.

Labeling Ideas for Bottled Gifts

A label on your homemade bottled gifts is not only a special touch, but is useful to identify the product, date made, and date to be used by — not to mention your name as maker! To get you started:

- Personalize the label with your name or the recipient's name or nickname.

- Use a photograph or illustration.

- Use rub-on lettering or stencils; or have labels typeset.

- If writing by hand, try colored ballpoint pens or permanent or metallic markers.

- Try adding borders or circle shapes.

Packaging Candies

Dress up homemade candies with attractive packaging. Stores which sell candy-making or cake decorating supplies (see Yellow Pages) sell fluted paper cups and folding boxes. Use baking cups for large pieces. Try a florist's or craft shop for unusual papers.

Package your individually wrapped candies in sand pails, balloon wine glasses, French jelly glasses, apothecary jars, coffee mugs, or whatever strikes your fancy.

Don't forget, during all the joyful preparation of your gifts, to save out enough for yourself and your family. May you all enjoy these lovely things too!

Place assorted marzipan fruits or vegetables on a pretty gift plate. Or nestle them in shredded cellophane; cover with plastic wrap, and top with a bow.

Giving fudge as a gift? Save yourself a mess: line gift boxes with wax paper or foil. Spray with nonstick spray. Let the fudge cool slightly; pour it directly into the boxes.

Packaging Potpourri

- For someone's living room give a large open bowl or shallow basket that holds three or four cupfuls of your best fragrance. Place your nicest dried flowers on the top.

- For a family room, fill a glass candy dish with a cover. Tell the recipient to remove the cover when she is in the room.

- Tuck potpourri bags behind couch and chair cushions. For a man's den, use fir balsam or spices. Citrus-spice is especially effective if smokers use the room. Cloves have long been the remedy for mustiness in trunks and drawers.

- Make lavender sachets to freshen clothes closets. Combine cedar with lavender for a sweeter aroma and moth repellence.

- Make simple fabric pouches without sewing. Cut an 8-inch circle or square of fabric and put half a cup of potpourri in the center. Gather the fabric up and tie with narrow ribbon. For closets, allow enough ribbon to make loops that may be slipped over a hanger.

- Every woman adores lacy sachets for her bureau drawers. Here is a way to concoct a lovely lace bag for gift giving. Buy a yard of ruffled lace 4 to 5 inches wide with a beading (small holes) along one edge. Cut a 6-inch piece and stitch the two ends together, then the bottom, to form a bag. Run ⅛-inch ribbon through the beading, starting at center front. Leave enough ribbon to tie a bow. Fill the bag with potpourri, tighten the ribbon, tie a nice bow, and there you are.

- For men's sock drawers choose a plaid or paisley fabric, and make a bag 4 inches square. Fill with an Oriental potpourri or Maine Woods Air.

- For a kitchen gift, make scented trivets or "hot pads" of 9-inch squares of fabric sewn into a pouch. Fill lightly with poly-fill, powdered orris root and a few drops of cinnamon oil. Close the end seam with hand stitches. Make mug mats the same way, using 6-inch squares or circles.

Material in this section has been excerpted and adapted from Making Liqueurs for Gifts *(A-101)*, Making and Using Flavored Vinegars *(A-112)*, Making Homemade Candy *(A-111)*, *and* Making Potpourri *(A-130)*, Storey/Garden Way Publishing Country Wisdom Bulletins.

List of Suppliers

Winemaking Suppliers

E.G. Arthurs & Sons, Ltd.
2046 Avenue Road
Toronto, ON
Canada M5M 4A6

The Complete Winemaker
1219 Main Street
St. Helena, CA 94574

Danenberger
Food Market
P.O. Box 276P
New Berlin, IL 62670

Great Fermentations
87 Larkspur Street
San Rafael, CA 94901

Oak Barrel Winecraft
1443 Pablo Avenue
Berkeley, CA 94702

Semplex of U.S.A.
4159 Thomas Avenue North
Minneapolis, MN 55430

Wine-Art of San Diego
460 Fletcher Parkway
El Cajon, CA 92020

Sourdough Suppliers

Goldrush Sourdough Starter is available in retail kitchen/gift stores.

Walnut Acres Starter is available through:
Walnut Acres
Penns Creek, PA 17862
Toll-free: 1-800-433-3998

Potpourri Suppliers

The Herb and Spice Collection
P.O. Box 118
Norway, IA 52318-0118

This thick catalog is free for the asking. Not only do they offer oils and botanicals for potpourri, but many other herbs and herbal products.

Create Something Special Catalog
Lorann Oils
4518 Aurelius Road
P.O. Box 22009
Lansing, MI 48909

A catalog to serve candy makers more than potpourri makers. You will not find rose petals or lavender here, but they handle an excellent line of oils including some that are hard to find elsewhere. Free.

Tom Thumb Workshops
Route 13
P.O. Box 357
Mappsville, VA 23407

From them you can buy oils and botanicals for potpourri, also their own potpourri blends. They also sell craft accessories and crafted gift items. Send long self-addressed stamped envelope with request.

Home Sew
Bethlehem, PA 18018-0140

The best mail order source we know for lace, ribbon, notions. Free catalog and prompt service.

Dody Lyness
Potpourri Party Line
7336 Berry Hill
Palos Verdes Peninsula, CA 90274

Dody has been making potpourri for many years. She not only publishes a quarterly newsletter, but also sells (at very good prices) high quality dried flowers, other botanicals and spices, and high quality oil. Please send a long self-addressed stamped envelope when requesting her price list.

Index

Lavender potpourri, 133
Lemon balm, 128
Lemon basil tea bread, 82
Lemon buttercream, 105
Lemon cream cheese pie, 93
Lemon peel, 129
Lemon verbena, 128
Licorice liqueur, 63
Lime buttercream, 105
Liqueur making, 56–58
Liqueurs
    bottling, 149
    with cherries, 105
Lye, 114–15

Malt syrup, 95
Maple syrup, 95
Maple-walnut buttercream, 104–5
Marmalade making, 12
Marzipan, 106–7
Medicated soap, 118–19
Melody potpourri, 137
Mennonite upside-down cake, 89
Middle eastern cauliflower pickles, 28
Mint buttercream, 105
Mixed-wax candles, 121
Molasses, 95
Molasses taffy, 108
Molded candles, 119–20, 122
Mothproofing sachet, 139
Mulberry jam, 10
Mustard pickles, 20
Myrrh, 130

No-cook refrigerator pickles, 25
Nut brittle, 99
Nutmeg, 129

Oakmoss, 129
Oatmeal soap, 118
Old-fashioned filled cookies, 91
Onion vinegar, 68
Orange buttercream, 105
Orange liqueur, 59
Orange peel, 106, 129
Orris root, 130

Packaging, 147–52
Parsnip wine, 52
Peach liqueur, 60
Peach melba jam, 10
Peach vinegar, 66
Peach vinegar pie, 96
Peaches, pickled, 28
Peanut brittle, 99
Peanut butter fondant, 109
Pear chutney, 31
Pears, pickled, 28
Peppermint liqueur, 63
Perfumed soap, 118
Perry, 51
Pickle making, 17–19
Pickled beets, 27
Pickled cabbage, 25
Pickled fruits, 25–31

Pickled vegetables, 25–31
Pickles, packaging, 148
Pies, 93–96
Pinchberry marmalade, 12
Pineapple jam, 9
Plum conserve, 12
Plum preserves, 15
Plum sauce, 32
Plum wine, 53
Potash lye, 114
Potato wine, 52
Potpourri
    freshening, 134
    packaging, 150
Potpourri making, 125–32
    recipes, 132–37
Pralines, 110
Preserve making, 14
Pretzels, 84
Pumpernickel bread, 78–79

Quick mustard pickles, 20
Quince honey, 13

Raisin bread, 79
Raspberry liqueur, 60
Raspberry vinegar, 66
Raspberry wine, 53
Red raspberry marmalade, 14
Refrigerator pickles, 24–25
Relish making, 17–19, 30–31
Rhubarb bars, 92
Rhubarb-raisin relish, 30
Rhubarb-strawberry pie, 94
Rolled candles, 120, 121–22
Rose geranium, 128
Rose hip jam, 10
Rose potpourri, 132–33
Rose soap, 118
Rosemary, 128
Rosemary-tarragon vinegar, 67
Rosy red pie, 95
Rosy rhubarb jam, 9
Rye bread, 78

Salt water taffy, 109
Sandalwood soap, 118
Sauces, 32–33
Scuppernong jam, 10
Seven-pepper vinegar, 69
Shallot vinegar, 68
Silver-scented geranium cake, 90
Simple sour cream cake, 88
Soap making, 111–19
Soda lye, 114
Solar-cooked jam, 8
Sorghum syrup, 95
Sour cherry jelly, 5
Sour cream cake, 88
Sour pickles, 22
Sourdough cherry cobbler, 89
Sourdough chocolate cake, 86–87
Sourdough making, 71–74
    recipes, 75–76, 78–79, 80, 83, 84,
        86–87, 89

Sourdough pretzels, 84
Sourdough pumpernickel, 78–79
Sourdough sesame crackers, 83
Sourdough white sandwich bread, 75
Sourdough zucchini bread, 80
Spearmint, 128
Spiced apples, 29
Spiced pickled cabbage, 25
Springsong potpourri, 137
Squash pie, 94
Star anise, 128
Stearin candles, 121
Strawberry preserves, 16
Sugar substitutes, 95
Sugar syrup, 58
Suppliers, 151–52
Sweet flag, 129
Sweet gherkins, 20
Sweet green wheels, 26
Sweet marjoram, 128
Sweet pickled peaches, 28
Sweet pickled pears, 28
Sweet woodruff, 128

Taffy, 108–9
Tallow candles, 120–21
Tarragon pickles, 24
Thousand island dressing, 33
Tomato chutney, 31
Tomato dills, 24
Tomato-pear preserves, 15
Tomatoes, pickled, 26
Tonka bean, 129
Transparent soap, 117
Truffles, 107

Uva-ursi, 128

Vanilla bean, 129
Vanilla caramels, 102
Vanilla fudge, 102
Vanilla pecan liqueur, 61
Vetiver, 129
Vinegar bottling, 149
Vinegar making, 64–65

Watermelon rind pickles, 29
Watermelon rind preserves, 15
Wheat wine, 53
White wine, 49
Whole wheat bread, 76–77
Wild cherry marmalade, 12
Wine bottling, 149
Winemaking, 35–53, 54–56
Wintergreen buttercream, 105
Woods potpourri, 134–35

Yogurt, substituting for cream cheese,
    90
Yogurt berry pie, 93

Zesty rye bread, 78
Zucchini bread, 80
Zucchini relish, 30–31